T0145136

OVERCOMING ODDS AND OBSTACLES:

The Story of A State Championship Team

Michael D Kurtz, D Min, LMFT

Also, by Michael D. Kurtz

Everyday Life in the Times of the Judges, Included in Abingdon's Bible Teacher Kit

Approaching the New Millennium: Biblical End-Time Images

Lessons From a Christmas Tree Farm: A Devotional and Study Guide Resource

Crossings: Memoirs of a Mountain Medical Doctor

Michael's Musings: A Pastor Blogs on Life

Mentoring Pew Sitters into Servant Leaders

iUniverse books may be ordered through booksellers or by contacting:

iUniverse
1663 Liberty Drive
Bloomington, IN 47403
www.iuniverse.com
844-349-9409

Because of the dynamic nature of the Internet, any web addresses or links contained in this book may have changed since publication and may no longer be valid. The views expressed in this work are solely those of the author and do not necessarily reflect the views of the publisher, and the publisher hereby disclaims any responsibility for them.

Any people depicted in stock imagery provided by Getty Images are models, and such images are being used for illustrative purposes only.
Certain stock imagery © Getty Images.

ISBN: 978-1-6632-5776-5 (sc)
ISBN: 978-1-6632-5775-8 (e)

Library of Congress Control Number: 2023922063

Print information available on the last page.

iUniverse rev. date: 11/20/2023

"My brothers and sisters, think of the various tests you encounter as occasions for joy. After all, you know that the testing of your faith produces endurance. Let this endurance complete its work so that you may be fully mature, complete, and lacking nothing" (James 1:2-4).

THE ASHE CENTRAL SCHOOL SONG

High upon the Blue Ridge Mountains

There's a place we love.

And we live there always seeking,

Higher aims above.

This the school of which we're proud,

We cherish with all our might.

This we sing our alma mater,

To our black and white.

For it's rah-rah for Central, Central

Rah-rah for Central, Central,

Rah-rah for Central,

Go…Win…Fight!

CONTENTS

Dedicated to the citizens of Ashe County, North Carolina, a people of strong independence and great resilience. The 1965 championship team is one example of this admirable independence and resilience.

FOREWORD

I have been asked many times how we won a state championship. I have always replied, it was the result of several things:

- Great talent, good size, and superb quickness
- Positive leadership
- Focus on fundamentals.
- Good character
- Team play – The players believed that the team was more important than any one individual. This made them very coachable.
- Finally, we had an advantage. We had a sixth man on the floor that gave us a reason to win. That sixth man was Wade Rose. While Coach Rose was in the hospital we were on the court. Wade was one of the finest coaches and individuals I have ever known. He was an excellent role model. He was an ardent student of the game of basketball. And he was my friend.

I was honored to be a part of the 1965 state champions. The team consisted of a great group of guys who bonded and banded together to bring a championship title to Ashe County. Our path to the crown was not an easy one. We faced challenges and obstacles all along the way. Yet we pulled together and persevered for the school, for the County, and for the "sixth man Coach."

On the following pages, my friend Michael Kurtz, with the help of many, has chronicled the journey of the 1965 Ashe Central High School Panthers to a state championship. I count it a privilege to have coached such a committed and courageous team.

Coach Morris Walker, 2023

ACKNOWLEDGMENT

I am grateful to many people who helped in making the book, "OVERCOMING ODDS AND OBSTACLES: The Story of A State Championship Team" into a reality. Coach Morris Walker, Gwen Rose Ashley and Charlie Bowers, who were each integral and important participants in this Ashe Central athletic anthology, made themselves available for many contacts and inquiries as concerns descriptions and details of the 1965 ACHS Championship Team.

There were many others, too many to mention here by name, who provided a plethora of pertinent information through interviews in person, and through phone calls. Others gave feedback and insights from their firsthand experiences with the '65 Panthers. Thanks to all for your excellent assistance with this endeavor of seeking to capture and chronicle a significant chapter in Ashe County history!

INTRODUCTION

I was a ten-year-old student at Jefferson Elementary School when the Ashe Central High School (ACHS) Panthers won the 1965 2A state basketball championship. My best friend's dad took us to the championship contest in Winston-Salem, N.C. We all watched with awe as the game clock ticked down the last seconds during the final game, and our guys were leading by double figures. This great win was an amazing accomplishment not only for the Team, but for the entire county of Ashe!

As the players returned home to numerous congratulations and various celebrations, they became local hometown heroes. Many of us younger kids sought to emulate some of the team members on the championship squad. At the neighborhood basketball goals, we worked on our game, pretending we were participating in the championship contest. As a player on the Ashe Central H. S. boys' varsity basketball team, during the early '70s, I was thrilled when I was assigned number fifty! No one had to remind me that Bob Francis had worn that number on the championship team.

What the 1965 Panthers pulled off was, without a doubt, a rarity. The odds of winning a state championship even under the best of circumstances, with all factors involved going your way, are extremely difficult and seldom attained. Yet the '65 Team accomplished this against-all-odds feat while overcoming overwhelming obstacles.

This book recaps the elation and celebration of a victorious high school squad. This writing also relates the heartaches and hardships the ACHS Team encountered along the journey, and which they countered with courage, unity and perseverance. The narrative is relayed through seven chapters. Yet, it is readily acknowledged, the enormity of this extraordinary enterprise – that of winning a state championship against all odds – cannot be totally captured through paper and pen. To a large degree, this is a location story. In other words, to truly assimilate this historical event, you had to be there!

Chapter one affirms that the 1965 state championship was not only an Ashe Central High School accomplishment. It was an Ashe County win. When the Panthers headed to postseason play, people and groups from throughout the County were supportive. Many even shared in a collective pride for a relatively small high school from their small, mountainous home taking on and defeating the flatlander favorites. The Team heard pejorative comments from opponent teams' fans who referred to the Panthers as "hillbilly hicks who probably won't last too long in the playoffs." This kind of mean-spirited rhetoric only served to further deepen and consolidate the resolve and unity of Ashe Countians.

In chapter two we give a look at the two coaches who guided and directed the cagers to their thrilling victory. These two men had a remarkably close relationship. Their respect for one another went deep. Both coaches were super competitive and high achievers throughout their careers as both players and coaches. Yet, far beyond athletic competition, both these men strove to be positive role models for their team and for others. In their eyes, values such as integrity, self-discipline and perseverance were not lofty, removed goals. Instead, these were attainable ethical practices to be lived, not perfectly, but, on a consistent basis, manifested in and through daily interpersonal relationships. Therefore, beyond the team members being groomed to become talented ball players, they were expected to be persons of integrity and positive citizens of the broader society. Before winning games on the floor, there was a call to practice winning ways in life, through self-discipline, integrity and respect, both for self and for others.

The Team players are the topic of chapter three. Fourteen players comprised the Panthers' squad. Each player contributed his specific skill set to the court, whether in the game or at practice. Each person on the team added his own individual personality to the total team temperament. What resulted was a unique team identity which enabled and empowered the Panther's to do something very few teams have ever done.

Teams don't win championships by themselves, on their own. It takes a village. Ask any of the players and they will quickly tell you that they had encouragement and support from many folks. The support of family, fans, friends and community forms the content of chapter four. A foundation of widespread affirmation and assistance helped to bolster and boost the 1965 championship team.

In chapter five, we are reminded no prize is ever won without paying a price. Likewise, no championship comes without a cost. The hurdles and hardships of hoops encountered by the Panthers, like for any team, would either make them or break them.

The support of the fan base was perhaps most publicly witnessed in the stands at the games. Busloads came from Ashe County to cheer on their Team. Chapter six's topic is "The Games." The six post-season games of the '65 championship will be highlighted and reviewed.

Finally, chapter seven celebrates the reality of a dream come true! It all comes down to one final game. Four quarters. Two halves. One winner, crowned champion. On the night of Saturday, March 13, 1965, the Ashe Central Panthers were named the North Carolina state 2A champions of high school basketball!

CHAPTER ONE

THE COUNTY

"I haven't seen this many people out in Ashe County since the railroad came to town!" Player Bob Francis recalls hearing this statement from an elderly citizen upon returning from the state championship game.

Ashe County, North Carolina is tucked away in the northwest corner of the state. The Ashe County Chamber of Commerce promotes Ashe as, "The Coolest Corner of North Carolina."

My parents migrated from the Northwestern portion of The United States to Ashe County during the summer of 1956. It was on my first birthday. I count this family transition as one of the best birthday gifts ever! From my perspective, Ashe County IS the "coolest corner" - - a relatively cool climate; cool-looking scenery; and, populated with very cool people.

Not everyone feels the same positive vibes toward Appalachian areas, such as Ashe. Some would call us highlanders "hillbillies." Some folks through the years have derided us as people who are "behind the times," or, "barefoot people who don't have in-door plumbing and who do not have a clue about a sophisticated, meaningful lifestyle."

During the ACHS first game of the North Carolina State 2A playoffs, against Stedman High School, two female fans from Stedman were discussing the outcome of the Ashe Central-Stedman game. A portion of their conversation went as follows, "Who are we playing tonight. Do you think we should reserve a hotel room for tonight?" "Oh, I don't think we'll have a problem. It's just some little high school up in the hills. We should be fine." One of the Panther's parents, Spencer Howell, seated in the bleachers behind these two ladies, overheard their comments. Spencer leaned over their shoulders and remarked, "Ladies, I don't think you need to bother with unpacking your suitcases tonight!"

Ashe County citizens have at times, over the years, considered themselves looked down upon when it comes to receiving their share of respect. And overlooked when the topic is State funding and resources. The coffers out of Raleigh seem to exhaust prior to making their offers reach this far west. Sometimes we have felt like we are in last place when the topic is allocation of state funds. At times it seems as if we are bypassed and neglected.

Perhaps it is our size. We are relatively small in population. The 1960 census reported fewer than 20,000 residents in Ashe County. Over the past sixty years we have only grown by an approximate seven thousand residents (Estimated population for 2022 stands at 27,110). Maybe it is our geographic location. We are nestled in the farthest northwest corner, bordering the Virginia and Tennessee state lines. Then, too, it could be about our history. We were part of what was called "The Lost Province." For a considerable amount of time, we were considered a separate state, or entity.

Could it be that our "Lost Province" status and identity helped shape a fierce independence and a strong resiliency that enable folks to persevere even through bone-chilling winters, economic challenges and feeling like the "state stepchild"? Maybe our relatively isolated territory and mountainous terrain, resulting in at least decades of a shortage of good highways in and out of Ashe, accounted for a feeling of separateness and a mindset of not being totally validated and included by many of the State powers that be.

Still, against many odds and despite many obstacles Ashe Countians have survived, and often thrived amid great challenges. When times get tough, as is often stated, the tough get going. The mountain motto could well be stated as, "We don't give up during hard times. We don't quit. We find a way to persevere. We will come through. And we will come through stronger together!"

A microcosm of this Ashe County perseverance and resiliency is observed in the account of a small mountain high school basketball team which won a state championship during the mid-1960s. In many ways, this unlikely and unique story seems like a "David and Goliath" narrative. Small takes on the bigs. An under-resourced group challenges the much more privileged programs. Players in blue jeans and letter jackets disembark off a well-worn activity bus, while watching their opponents arrive in deluxe coach buses.

And like "David," the much smaller school from the high country – "the hillbillies" – were often discounted and even derided by their opponents. Roger Howell, a member of the '65 Team recounted an example of this derision toward the Panthers, as they checked into their hotel stay for the tournament, "The other three schools were already there. They had big greyhound buses with school logos, and they had blazers.

They started giving us a hard time because we had old blue jeans on and A-club jackets. They were hollering for us to 'get back to the sticks.' Coach Walker wouldn't let us say nothing. He said, 'we'll take care of things tonight.' And we did."

After the Panther Team had been bad-mouthed and derided as "hillbillies" all week long during the entire state tournament, they did take care of business on the court, keeping their mouths closed while their game did the talking. However, they had taken about all the verbal abuse any team could stand. On Saturday night, after Central had won the State Championship, and the Panthers were getting on their team bus, one of the players rushed over to the nearby opponent's bus, who they had just defeated for the championship, and shouted out, "Go home to the Sandhills!" Oh well, no one is perfect, and all are fallible, including the Panther players!

The courageous and victorious narrative of the 1965 Ashe Central High School state championship in the sport of basketball is more than a single school story. It is the account of an entire County. The team represented the best of a mountain mentality of determination, perseverance and unity. It is a story of pulling together especially during hard times.

The topography of Ashe County consists of mountain peaks reaching above five thousand feet in elevation, with The Peak of Creston claiming the highest height at 5,150 feet. There are numerous scenic mountains populating the landscape. Some of these Appalachian hills are rugged and make for difficult climbs to their summits. But for those who navigate and persevere in the climb the resulting vista views are greatly rewarding!

The County of Ashe also inhabits beautiful wide valleys within its borders. These valleys are often nestled at the base of several mountains. For example, the valley town of West Jefferson is located between the mountains known as Mount Paddy, Mount Jefferson and Phoenix Mountain. Or, again, for instance, The Clifton valley community, with the North Fork of the New River flowing through this territory, is found at the base of Three Top Mountain.

Gorgeous, rugged, and strenuous to climb, these Blue Ridge Mountains reach to the sky. And wide, level terrain valleys, often contain pastures of green with gently flowing rivers. On the hillsides one will often observe Christmas trees growing. In the valleys it is common to see cattle grazing.

Ashe County is the land of Christmas trees, beef cattle and country living. In this rural, remote and mountainous milieu one is likely not surprised to see the agricultural beauty and bounty. However, to view exemplary athletic accomplishments may not be peoples' first thought while traveling and traversing through the pastoral and agricultural countryside. Probably few, if any, outsiders consider Ashe a land that has yielded State basketball champions.

Yet, athletic excellence has been, and is currently, evidenced in this County. Furthermore, a state championship vision was formed, fashioned and came to fruition in this coolest corner of North Carolina. That championship team was the 1965 Ashe Central Panthers. The Panthers championship narrative, in many ways, parallels the County terrain from where they resided, with its rugged, strenuous to climb, mountain ridges and highly elevated ranges, coupled with its valleys of flowing waters and fertile land. The '65 Team went through some low valleys on their march. They encountered the strenuous struggles of climbing and persevering through extreme adversity. They went through some deep valleys. They also experienced the enormous ecstasy of climbing and making it to the top of the final summit. Succinctly stated, the Championship Team during the '64-'65 season went through some valleys and climbed some steep elevations on their way to being crowned 2A State champions.

The Panthers' season was filled with peaks and valleys. Ashe County folks had raised, rallied behind, and were rewarded by, a group of young athletes who, with a lot of county support and encouragement, made it to the summit of their sport. They had climbed to the very top of the highest tournament, the state!

In 2008, the 1965 Ashe Central Team was inducted into the Ashe County Sports Hall of Fame, further evidencing the County connection and recognition. Their place in the County's sports history and athletic legacy was permanently solidified.

In the pages and chapters which follow is presented the inspiring account of a group of high county guys, from a small school in a small town, taking on, and taking out, the giants. They overcame the obstacles. They beat the odds.

Ashe County's terrain contains many majestic mountains alongside a variety of verdant valleys. Pictured here is The Peak, at Creston, N C. The highest elevation in Ashe County is recorded at the summit of The Peak.

CHAPTER TWO

THE COACHES

"It really helped the team that Coach Rose and Coach Walker were close friends." – Player Dickie Bower

"A coach's primary responsibility is not only to make better players, but to make better people." – Coach John Wooden

To know the character and the chemistry of the 1965 championship team look at the coaches who coached them. As with any team, coaches set the posture, tone and style for their players. Players take their cues from their coaches, whether positive or negative. Coaches design, develop and delegate strategies for athletic contests. They also guide and influence the behaviors and emotions of their players through both example and education. Example is critical for congruity and to avoid hypocrisy. As has been said, "more is caught than taught." There are at least four central characteristics required of good coaches. All four elements are essential if one hopes to foster a strong and successful team. These characteristics could be referred to as "The four Cs of coaching."

The first characteristic is COMPETENCE. The coach needs to have people skills and the coach needs to know the game. That is, the coach needs to have and demonstrate relationship knowledge along with possessing insights pertaining to the fundamentals and the strategies of the specific sport being coached.

Second, the coach must display and relay CONFIDENCE to the team members. Coaches need to believe in themselves, in their team players and in their strategies and execution of those strategies. Belief in the team and in their potential breeds confidence that is contagious. Laying out a vision, along with a structure and strategy to follow and fulfill that stated vision, is vital to team confidence building. This is a major role of coaches, to project confidence and to instill a sense of confidence in the entire team.

Third, the coach needs to facilitate and foster functional and supportive CONNECTIONS within the team, as well as positive and helpful connections with other people and resources outside the team and within the local community. As used here "connections" refer to good chemistry, unity, evidenced in team relationships. It is helpful to remember that unity is oneness, but not sameness. Authentic unity respects and utilizes the different and various individual talents of each of the team members, while integrating and adjusting those talents for the sake of the entire team. Individual recognition and nurture are important, yet the team's group identity and goals become paramount.

Fourth, positive and trustworthy coaches need to be people of good CHARACTER. They should be individuals of integrity. Integrity does not imply perfection. There are no perfect coaches, for there are no perfect people. People of integrity do their very best, and when they do not achieve their goals and expectations, they admit their shortcomings. They take responsibility for their behavior. They own up to their mistakes and they own their failures when they occur. A coach's integrity also includes respect and advocacy for their players. They look out for the holistic well-being of their players, first and foremost as human beings.

The 1964-65 Panthers were extremely fortunate to have not only one coach who possessed and practiced the "four C's" of coaching, but two coaches who lived out these values. Any team would be enormously blessed to locate and to acquire and hire a coach who lives out these positive coaching characteristics. But to have two coaches with these much-desired qualities on the same bench at the same time is extremely rare. Two high-capacity coaches, and more importantly, two high-caliber individuals of positive character coached the '65 champions.

COACH WADE ROSE
(November 20, 1936 – March 15, 1965)

Wade Rose was raised in the eastern part of Ashe County, in the Glendale Springs community. His parents were the late Delmer and Helen Rose. The Roses owned and operated a store in Glendale Springs. When Gwen Rose Ashley was asked to describe her former in-laws she replied, "Delmer was a very good, reliable man. He was the quieter of the two. Helen was more extrovertive. She was fun and loved to joke with folks."

Wade grew up playing ball. He loved sports. He was most happy when he had a basketball in his hands. He was motivated and driven by athletic competition. And, truth told, his athletic interest and love of sports paid dividends. He attended Jefferson High School, playing on the school team, and helped the team to win the 1952-53 Ashe County Championship. Following high school graduation in 1954, the same year he was named a member of the All-Northwest Team, Rose was awarded a basketball scholarship to Lees-McRae Junior College in Banner Elk, N.C. While at LMC (1954-1956) Rose was the '55-'56 Co-Captain, and was honorable mention: All-State Junior College, 1956. Upon graduating from Lees-McRae he transferred to Catawba College (1956-1958) in Salisbury, N.C., where he played two years of basketball.

During Wade's college years, Gwen Neal, a native of Jefferson, and Rose were married. When asked, "What would you tell us about Wade as a person?" she replied, "Well, above all he loved his family. And he taught us about Christian living and playing, and about Christian dying,"- - alluding to his lifestyle of integrity and referring to his relatively young age (age 28) of dying, yet with definite dignity.

She continued describing Coach Rose. "He was a prankster. He loved to play jokes on others, and on me." The first year we were married he said, 'I got you something. I wrapped it, but I'm afraid you won't like it. I shopped around for it, but I just don't think you'll really like it!' So, with great anticipation I unwrapped and opened the large box. What I pulled out was a very large, tacky, olive-green ballroom dress, which looked like it had been worn during the "Gone with the Wind" era! It was awful! But it got us both laughing."

On another occasion, when Wade was teaching and coaching at Ashe Central High School, Gwen (Mrs. Rose when this occurred) was volunteering, assisting the secretary in the school office. As it was approaching Valentine's Day, she was addressing some Valentine cards. During third period a female student approached Gwen and handed her an envelope, "Coach says to give this to you." When she opened the envelope, right away she recognized that Wade had hijacked one of her cards. Inside, the card read, "Happy Valentine's Day to an especially good friend." He signed the card, "From a secret admirer, Coach Rose."

Gwen and Wade were good for each other. They held similar beliefs and commitments when it came to foundational values such as their Christian faith, a caring, supportive family, and a strong work ethic. At the same time, they provided a balance in personality for one another. Gwen was more studious, she even helped Wade with his academic papers. He was more carefree and even absent-minded at times. On one occasion, while visiting family, Wade drove off and forgot to bring Gwen with him. His mind, Gwen recounted, was likely on basketball.

Gwen was more organized and structured. Wade was the prankster of the two. While she was more apt to stay focused on accomplishing the day-to-day tasks and chores which family life requires, Coach Rose was more spontaneous. and a dreamer. Together they were a committed, complementary team.

Their marital teamwork and complementary talents were evident especially during basketball season. While Wade coached, Gwen often cooked and was a gracious hostess. Many meals were served and enjoyed by team members in the Rose home. In fact, she recalls, "Our home often became like a second home to the players. Sometimes they would stay at our place overnight. We enjoyed their company, and, in addition, we knew where they were and what they were doing. Our three young children, Mary, Ginny and John, experienced the high school boys as if they were older brothers. In many ways, the young men were more like family than like a team. In fact, I'm convinced this closeness and accountability that developed greatly contributed to their success on the basketball floor."

Coach Rose coached several of the '65 champions for six years, beginning in the seventh grade at Jefferson Elementary School and culminating in their senior year at Ashe Central High School. This core group of players knew well his philosophy and expectations. They were schooled early on in basketball fundamentals, as Rose was a stickler for the basics of the sport. As mentioned earlier, Wade was not a top-notch student in the classroom. And he could be a scatter brain at times. Yet, when it came to basketball, he was a totally focused student of the game. He was anything but absent-minded as concerned practice routines and game strategies.

In fact, Coach Rose always kept a small red notebook with him during the season. In this well-preserved book is found the following:

- The current season schedule.
- Reminder notes for additional teams to put on schedule.
- Orders for players' shoes, game socks and warmups.
- Rule changes for boys' high school basketball.
- Rough copies of recommendation letters to send to colleges on behalf of current team players.
- Pre-game menu items for a stronger performance.
- A list of players assigned uniform numbers and locker numbers.
- Offense principles for the team.
- A list of miscellaneous basketball principles.
- Some essential game rules.
- Rough copies of letters to former players.

Following are some excerpts from Coach Rose's red notebook:

AN EXAMPLE OF A ROUGH DRAFT OF A RECOMMENDATION LETTER

Bucky Waters

Assistant Basketball Coach

Duke University

Durham, North Carolina

Dear Bucky,

After recovering from another operation, I am back in school. The doctors are hopeful that things will be alright for, at least, awhile.

I am told you might be available one night maybe to talk to my boys or possibly work with a few of them. We have a fellow-Bob Francis-that has lots of college potential. We have another prospect which would bear looking at. He is a 6'5" junior recruit. He is a fine prospect.

Hope to see you soon. We will again be following the Blue Devils and wish you continued success.

Sincerely,

Wade Rose

COACH ROSE'S RECOMMENDED PRE-GAME MENU

- Boiled potatoes
- Baked potatoes
- Hamburger
- Steak
- Boiled chicken
- Beef stew
- Baked ham

- Oyster stew
- Broiled fish
- Soups
- Small amount of white bread
- Crackers
- Fruit salads
- Tea
- One glass of sweet milk
- Small amount of ice cream
- Avoid fried, greasy foods and sweets.

COACH ROSE'S MISCELLANEOUS GAME PRINCIPLES

- Play percentages – look for a good shot.
- Always follow shot to basket.
- Be able to control the ball for a long period of time.
- Never shoot when someone closer to the basket is open.
- Never shoot until rebounders are near basket.
- Know the plays and do your part.
- Strive for perfection in teamwork.
- Never "hog" the ball.
- Use bounce passes underneath basket.
- Faking is necessary in any offense.
- Never take unnecessary chances.
- Always keep at least one player at safety position.
- Never rush a set offense.
- Accept everything as a challenge.

From these "red book" details, and from much feedback provided by players and observers, it is abundantly clear that Coach Rose had developed a clear vision for his team members, and for the team. He also provided a structure and strategies which enabled the players, and ultimately the team, to succeed in great ways. From coaching and instilling a philosophy and an expectation in a core group of athletes beginning in elementary school, and then continuing together in high school; from integrating other players who eventually joined the Panther team; from dwelling on basketball fundamentals; from teaching miscellaneous principles of the game; from exemplifying a commitment to, and support of, each individual player; and, from even guiding their dietary habits for optimal performance and health; from all these ingredients and more, Coach Rose had a recipe for excellent results. If the team members would follow his vision and his structure which undergirded the vision, the odds would be good for success.

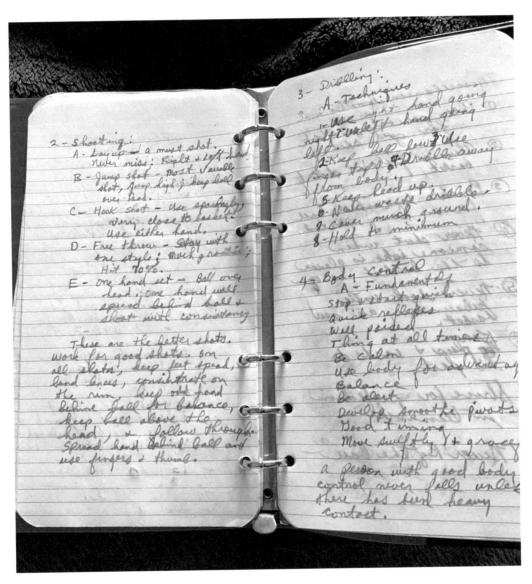

Coach Rose's Red Book

The Panthers team had an extraordinarily excellent coach in Wade Rose. It was his vision and his commitment to steadfastly follow this vision, even amid extreme adversity, that shaped and bolstered this team. It was his respect and care shown to his players that won their loyalty and confidence. Wade Rose was a coach who promoted and practiced the "4Cs" of coaching – competence, confidence, connections and character.

PLAYER COMMENTS ON COACH ROSE

I first met Coach Rose in middle school where I briefly played with many of the guys who later formed the ACHS State Championship team. During summer visits to my grandparents in Ashe County, I reconnected with the team and frequently played basketball. Coach Rose stayed in contact with me from eighth grade through my sophomore year and frequently asked me to consider returning to North Carolina to be part of his team. He had a vision even at this early time that his team would do great things. Coach Rose was one of the strongest men that I have ever known. The day I returned to Ashe County, I went to the miniature golf course (Put and Putt in Jefferson) and Coach Rose came across the bridge using a cane to walk. His face was beaming, and he expressed excitement that I had come back to join his team. Coach Rose stated that I provided the "missing link" that he envisioned for the team. He remained actively coaching as long as humanly possible and never complained. – David Mullis

When asked, "What would you say about Coach Rose as a coach," Wade's widow, Gwen responded, "He loved the boys like they were his own. He was always an advocate for his players." -Gwen Rose Ashley (Wife of Coach Rose)

"'The fine nine,' as Coach Rose called us, began in the seventh grade at Jefferson Elementary School. That was when our team started our march to the championship. Coach Rose and his wife Gwen took us under their wings and from then on, we were his team. Our team did everything together from baseball to ping pong to bowling to tennis, and especially basketball. We practiced basketball the year round including "summer camp," which was probably considered illegal by the North Carolina High School Athletic Association! If truth be told, Coach Rose did not want us to play football, as football would take time away from basketball, as well as pose a better chance of being injured. My parents were very pleased with me not playing football!" – J. Michael "Mike" Badger

I first remember Coach Rose when I was in the 7th grade. He was one of the nicest and most respectful individuals I had ever met. He also could beat us in every and any game. He was great at croquet, although I think he may have made up rules from time to time. He was a great coach. He never used foul language or really fussed at us much. He would give us pointers on how to improve without being critical. He only fussed at us if we did not hustle. I spent a good deal of time in Glendale Springs at the home of Coach and Gwen Rose. He always encouraged us to dress nicely. Our junior and senior years we had nice black blazers to wear to the games. I worked at his Put and Putt mini golf course for a few years, and Coach Rose was also great at mini golf! – Lanney Blevins

Coach Rose was the best athlete I have ever seen! He was some special kind of basketball player. There were some summer pickup games in which he participated. Coach was faster, could jump higher, shoot better, and out rebound the others. Lord help you, if you had to guard him man-to-man! All the things he was teaching us to do in practice, he was doing in those pickup games. It made you want to do it like he did. Coach Rose taught us many positive values, such as hard work. Before our practices started in high school each season we had to run to get in shape. We had never done that before. Also, we were required to come to the gym and help him strip the basketball floor and resurface it every year. And no one was allowed on that floor without basketball shoes! The take-away messages? Take care of your stuff. Put in the work necessary to keep things in order." – Dickie Bower

He (Coach Rose) not only taught us basketball. He taught us about life in general, including how to behave. He was a great person who set a great example! – The late Roger Howell from an interview with Josh Beckworth

Coach Wade Rose with the Jefferson Elementary Team

COACH MORRIS WALKER
(Born November 14, 1937)

Morris Walker was raised in the western part of Ashe County, in the Warrensville community. His parents, the late Roy and Florence Walker, owned and operated a service station in Warrensville.

Morris grew up loving athletics. He played football, basketball and baseball at Lansing High School. In basketball he set many records and received numerous awards. In 1956 he was named to the All-Northwest Basketball Team, set the County record for most points scored in a men's single game (54 points), and had a scoring average of 32.6 points per game.

In 1959 Walker did his student teaching at Ashe Central High School. Morris reported to his supervising teacher. As he stood at the desk waiting for instructions the teacher finally acknowledged him and asked him what he wanted. When Walker stated he was assigned as his student teacher, the man replied, "I don't want or need a student teacher!"

Standing in the doorway, hearing everything, was teacher and coach Charles Moyer. Moyer immediately chimed in, "I need a student teacher." From that moment onward during his student teacher term, Morris was mentored by Moyer. Coach Moyer left Ashe Central that same year and Walker stepped in as teacher and coach. From 1960 through 1967, Morris coached football, basketball, baseball and golf at ACHS.

1967 was the debut for Coach Walker as the head coach of the Northwest Ashe High School Mountaineers. A portion of his coaching accomplishments at NWA included:

- District 7AA Northern Division Championship, 1968.
- District 7AA Championship, 1969.
- Made the NCHSAA State Tournament, 1969.

From teaching and coaching Walker transitioned to administrative roles in the Ashe County School System. From 1972-1989 he was principal of Northwest Ashe High School. Under his leadership NWA High School completed several improvements and projects, not the least which was the construction of a swimming pool which enabled swimming classes to be incorporated into the physical education curriculum. I was hired by Mr. Walker to teach English and coach boys' basketball and several other sports. I count it a privilege and blessing to have worked with Morris and the NWA staff and students for four years (1977-1981).

In 1989 Walker became the superintendent of Ashe County schools. He served ten years in this capacity, retiring in 1999. In his tenure as superintendent Morris received many recognitions and awards for his faithful service, seeking to advance the formal education of Ashe County students. In 1994 he was the recipient of the NCHSAA Superintendent of the Year.

As important as the educational career of serving others was to Walker, that which was closest to his heart was his family. In 1958 Morris and Katy Goodman were married. They were blessed with two children: Mitzi Walker Graves and Chuck Walker.

Katy was also an educator, serving as an English teacher and a media specialist. Katy and Morris worked together as a team, both in their school careers and in family life. While Morris was coaching basketball and other sports, Katy was coaching the cheerleaders. One year she made uniforms for each of the cheerleaders on the squad, as their athletic budget wasn't sufficient to purchase new ones.

Morris often second-guessed his ability at writing so Katy would come through and help with composing and editing communications and speeches. Katy, as an English major, evidenced high verbal skills and enjoyed expressing herself through writing. Another sign of teamwork.

Daughter Mitzi reflects, "Mom was the realist. For example, she would say, if you want to be a teacher, you're going to have to spend a lot of hours outside of class grading papers and preparing lesson plans." She went on to share, "Dad was the eternal optimist. He looked for, and found, the best in any situation."

Their son Chuck recalls, "Dad was not a complicated person. He had a simple philosophy which he taught us and which he lived. His number one rule: You do what is right. And in his educational career that simple and single philosophy translated to, you do what is right for the student."

Both Mitzi and Chuck remarked how during such demanding careers, with busy schedules, both their parents made time for family. Somehow, they managed to carve out time to gather each evening around the table for dinner together. Mitzi remembered how both parents attended every one of her home high school tennis matches. Chuck recalled how their parents attended his games, "Sometimes Dad would be leaning on his car, watching our team compete, prior to his rushing off to a school meeting. In fact, a lot of evenings, after Dad arrived home, while in his dress shirt and tie, he would hit the tennis ball with me in the backyard, prior to grabbing a quick bite with the family, then heading off to a school responsibility."

Mitzi also reflected, "One thing I especially appreciate about Dad is this: He was always the same. He provided a sense of calm, even-keeled, level-headedness. That helped many times to give me a sense of calm, sometimes in the middle of some chaos."

I can recall this calm temperament of Mr. Walker on display when I, as a teacher and coach on his Northwest Ashe High School staff, had just received my CDL, enabling me to drive an activity bus to take my athletic teams to away contests. I did a five-mile solo test with an activity bus. All went well. I navigated bridges and turns and intersections. I finished the trial run. Then it happened. As I was backing the bus into the school garage, I heard a scraping sound. I had backed through the garage door just fine. What I did not see was the iron beam in the middle of the parking bay. I placed an unwanted racing stripe down the side of the school's activity bus!

A first year, rookie teacher and coach. A blemished bus on my watch. What was I going to do? I called Morris. He came to the garage. He assessed the damage. Without raising his voice, he calmly stated, "These things happen. It will be alright. Not to worry. It's the old activity bus and it already has some scrapes and dents." What grace on display! The non-anxious presence which Morris displayed served to calm and relieve me.

A calm temperament and a steady disposition are very important qualities for a coach to practice and to display, as players take their cues from the coach. The higher the game stressors and the greater the anxiety in a contest, the greater the need for a steady, non-anxious presence, in order to foster focus and to bring calm to the center of chaos. With Coach Rose gravely sick and with the Panthers facing several opponents where they were considered underdogs, the stakes were high. No doubt anxieties were elevated. Overwhelming obstacles breed angst and anxiety. Morris Walker, assistant coach, now called during the '65 season to step up and take the reins, would present the kind of steady persona needed. The team had before them the opportunity to apply the many years of teaching and training from Coach Rose, and now coupled with the calm disposition and steady temperament of Coach Walker, to make something very special and unique happen.

Morris' history with, and under, Coach Rose, his own play and study of the game of basketball, and his upbringing through family and community, had prepared him for this unexpected and undesired turn of events. This was not what he and Coach Rose had planned. This was not the roadmap they had often discussed. Coach Rose was the head coach. Coach Walker the assistant. The coaching formula -Rose as head coach, Walker as assistant coach - felt good and right. But life has a way of throwing you curves, and when they come you adjust the best that you can with what you have. And during change and stress it is our bedrock values which guide our decision-making and our responses to, and through, tough choices. Pray you have developed the right values for such a time as this!

These are the kind of values ("Do what is right," commitment to family, serving the community, sacrificing for others, displaying an even-keeled temperament, etc.), decisions, and practices which shape responsible people, who become positive role models, investing in the lives of others for the good of culture and society. People like Coach Walker and Coach Rose.

Morris' value of commitment and his mantra "Do what is right," was sorely tested when his Katy began showing signs of memory impairment at the relatively early age of sixty-four! Just when a married couple is beginning to plan for and to reap and enjoy the fruits of their labors, in the season of retirement, an unforeseen loss and grief occurs. How would Katy be cared for? Yet, for Morris, there was no question about it. He would look after his soulmate and care for her every day. This he did, lovingly looking after her daily needs. This was his method of operation as long as he could physically maintain. The medical community assessed and intervened after years of his undivided care for his lifelong partner. Seeing Katy's condition and observing the toll taken on Morris, the tending physician said in no uncertain terms, "Mr. Walker, it is time now for you to place Katy in third party care, in a memory care facility, for her sake and for yours." For the final year of her life Katy resided in professional memory care. Yet, every day Morris would visit his teammate for life. Katy was lovingly cared for, and Morris had no regrets.

This commitment and deep care in and through difficult life circumstances is what builds positive character. As the words of scripture (Listed as a theme scripture on an opening page of this book), through the pen of James, relates, "My brothers and sisters, whenever you face trials of any kind, consider it nothing but joy, because you know that the testing of your faith produces endurance; and let endurance have its full effect, so that you may be mature and complete, lacking in nothing" (James 1:2-4).

Whether teaching, caring for Katy, or coaching, Morris brought a maturity to the table that provided security and a sense of calm to those within his realm of responsibility and care. For the 1965 Team this meant a positive guidance and care – a maturity – that was manifest beyond Coach Walker's years, for he was only in his late twenties. Relatively speaking, Morris was a very young coach, with limited coaching experience. Truth told; he was not all that much older than some of his players on the team!

Yet, he had learned, and gleaned, from a young age valuable lessons for life. At the inaugural Ashe County Sports Hall of Fame gathering in 2008, where both Coach Rose and Coach Walker were inducted into the Hall of Fame, Morris named three of the main influences in his life journey.

First, he recalled his parents, Roy and Florence Walker. "I grew up in a home with a lot of love and support. I was very fortunate to have this support and guidance in my life. They provided me with security and care. They also taught me a good work ethic. During the 1949-1950 academic year at Warrensville School, when I was twelve, my dad consulted with the teacher and suggested it would be good for me to have a job at the school. My first paid job was with the school, building fires each morning in the woodstove to heat the facility. My parents set expectations for me early on. They valued being responsible citizens in a community and doing your fair share of the work, along with others."

Second, Walker named Coach Charlie Stancil, who coached at Lansing School, as a lasting positive influence on his life. "Charlie Stancil was one of my coaches along the way. From him I learned, be in your best physical condition, play by the rules, and be a good role model for others."

Third, Morris reflected upon his relationship with Katy Goodman Walker, his wife. "One of the best decisions I ever made was beginning at age eleven, riding my bicycle from Warrensville to Smethport, and meeting on the church steps with Katy Goodman! I had my eyes on her, and thankfully she showed some reciprocation. I was blessed to call her my wife. She has been a true soulmate in the journey, and she never hesitated to give me her honest opinion and feedback, which, when heeded, probably spared me much heartache and regret."

The Panthers Team had a high-capacity person and coach in Morris Walker. The lessons he learned early on assisted him greatly in facing a difficult challenge, yet awesome opportunity. He was to be a lead coach for a team, which under devastating circumstances, had been handed off into his responsibility and care. Coach Walker provided a needed steady hand and a non-anxious presence for a group of guys, unbeknown to them, who were soon to experience some tough blows and, at the same time, some incredible victories.

PLAYER COMMENTS ON COACH WALKER

The hurdle to overcome was when our beloved Coach Rose was sick and diagnosed with lung and liver cancer. That made our team come together like no other team, playing for our dying coach. Coach Walker did a great job of coaching when Coach Rose was incapacitated. – Michael Badger

Coach Walker was such a supportive person to Coach Rose. He took over the coaching reins as Coach Rose's health prevented his active involvement. Walker was always cognizant that it was a team that Wade Rose had assembled and mentored since elementary school days. He never tried to make it his team but worked to bring out the best in each of us as players and young men. Since I was essentially an "outsider" joining the team in the final season of quest for the state championship, Coach Walker really made me feel welcome and appreciated. I think Coach Walker and I shared a common bond since we were both somewhat outsiders to the original core members of the state championship team. I will always be grateful for his kindness, leadership and friendship that has continued all these years.

After Coach Rose was unable to be on the team bench with us, Coach Walker was the glue that held us together. He kept us updated on Coach Rose's condition since he was in the hospital, and he kept us focused on the task before us. - David Mullis

When we went to Ashe Central High School in 1961, Coach Rose became the head coach and Coach Walker was the head football coach and assistant basketball coach. They were a great team together coaching. I was a manager for the football team for my junior and senior year for Coach Walker. –Lanney Blevins

Dickie Bower and I were the two that Coach Walker always had to keep an eye upon. We got to Winston-Salem for the state tournament and our room was the first one that Coach Walker came to and told us not to leave the room.

Coach Walker stepped in and helped us finish the trail that we were on. He taught me that you don't have to score twenty points a game to be a winner. He also taught me a lot of things about life. If it had not been for him, I don't know where I would be today. We have remained lifelong friends and I consider him part of my family and one of my best friends. – Eddie Vannoy

THE COACHES AS A TEAM

Coaches Rose and Walker

As mentioned earlier, the Championship Team was very fortunate to have two high-caliber, high-capacity coaches and individuals on the same bench at the same time – Head Coach, Wade Rose and Assistant Coach, Morris Walker. They both held similar values in life and parallel philosophies pertaining to coaching a team. In addition, these two men were friends, good friends. They enjoyed working together on the basketball court. And they appreciated time together outside of basketball.

When asked about his relationship with Rose, Walker affirmed, "I could not have found a better person, or better friend, in my life. Wade was a first-class kind of person. He possessed high values, yet he was down to earth, a person of genuine humility and grace. I very much cherish the time I had with him. I regret he left us so early."

There was a reciprocal respect between these coaches, a mutual admiration for one another. In a scrapbook Katy Walker had put together of the '65 team, there is contained a personal note which I was privileged to read. It is a note from Coach Rose to Coach Walker written in 1964, one year prior to Wade's death. The note reads:

Coach,

If there has ever been anyone I would like to be like and have admired; it is, you. There is no way I can say thank you for all you have done. If it was ever meant for me to be or to have a brother, I would want it to be Morris Walker.

Wade

As basketball players, Wade and Morris were opponents on the court, Rose played at Jefferson High School and Walker played at Lansing High School.   As high school players on the basketball floor they were on opposing sides, but as coaches they were on the same team, on the same bench and on the same wavelength with similar life and game philosophies. They worked as a team. They held deep respect for each other. They covered for one another. And adversity drew them even closer together.

On a school day in 1964 at Ashe Central High School all started as a normal academic day. Students and teachers were in their respective classrooms. Classes had changed a couple of times. Mr. Walker and Mr. Rose taught classes across the hallway from one another. During third period Coach Walker heard a lot of noise coming from Coach Rose's class. He instructed his class to work on their assignment and he walked across the hall to investigate the matter. Mr. Rose was absent from his class. Mr. Walker next headed to the coaches' office and what he found was disconcerting. Coach Rose was lying on the floor of the office. Rose was transported for medical attention. This is when it became public knowledge that the Coach was very sick. It turned out the diagnosis was liver cancer. He was provided with a portable medical pump that released antibiotics into his body to hopefully treat his malady. Coach Rose amazingly continued to coach as best he could with what energy he could muster. But the coaching became harder and harder to accomplish. Going forward the dynamic shifted. Wade often did much of the coaching through Morris, delegating and entrusting more and more responsibility and decision-making through his younger assistant.

This different and difficult coaching dynamic drew the men closer in their personal relationship. They seemed to both be aware of the brevity and sanctity of time. Not only did the coaches spend more time together, but when Coach Rose felt strong enough the two couples – Wade and Gwen and Morris and Katy - would get together for fellowship, food and the famous Rook games!

Gwen reflected, "Wade and Morris liked and enjoyed similar interests. Also, Katy and I liked the company of one another and became great friends. As two couples, we loved to play Rook."

When they played Rook, the guys played the gals. Morris remembers, "When Wade had the Rook, he would adjust his glasses with his middle finger. This was a signal we developed for 'card communication.' In addition, we learned where to always sit while playing against the ladies. I would sit in front of the cupboard with the glass so that Wade could see the reflection of my cards in the furniture."

A wonderful friendship bond developed between the two coaches. Similar upbringings. So many similar passions. So many similar values. A portion of these similarities follows:

- Both were raised in Ashe County.
- Both held status of "only child."
- Both came from families who served the community through commerce (a store and a service station respectively).
- Both were raised with the solid values of faith, family, hard work and integrity.
- Both loved athletics. Both excelled in basketball.
- Both were led to teaching and coaching at the high school level.
- Both had the philosophy of being role models for others.
- And both received at least one undeserved technical foul, as related below:

When playing the card game of Rook, Wade Rose had a habit of continually adjusting his eyeglasses with his middle finger. During a basketball game as Coach Rose was employing this habit it caught an official's attention. He thought the Coach was being derogatory, so the official gave him a technical foul. Morris recounts, "Honestly, Coach Rose did not deserve that technical. I was around him very much and this was his established method of securing his glasses. Wade looked at me after receiving this technical foul and asked what he got the penalty for? He truthfully did not know. He was a true gentleman."

Coach Walker had his own experience with an underserved technical foul while coaching the Northwest Ashe Mountaineers boys' basketball team. Morris had a player on his squad named Mack (many of us in Ashe County know and love Mack). Mack was bringing the ball up the court and apparently was not executing what Coach Walker had diagrammed during a timeout. Walker yelled at him, "Hey, Mack, get in the game!" One of the referees hit Coach Walker with a T, thinking he was screaming at the official.

Rose and Walker were both individuals of integrity and both were excellent coaches, and both had feet of clay, as does every human being. Their down-to-earth ways only made them more endearing and believable. What a relatable, caring, and talented tandem of coaches that led the 1965 Ashe Central Panthers! They both taught and displayed the "4Cs of Coaching" – competence, confidence, connections and, above all, character.

COMMENTS ON THE COACHES

The squad of '65 was a great basketball team, and all the players were a very close-knit group who rallied around Coach Rose even though he was unable to continue coaching. Coach Walker was faced with the task of continuing to coach and rally the players. He stepped into the position and did a masterful job. The players respected him and did everything he asked of them.

Coach Rose stressed the fundamentals of basketball and Coach Walker continued that legacy. The only game they lost that year was to North Wilkes at North Wilkes. North was a very talented team. After the loss on the activity bus, the team was returning to Ashe County and some of the players were laughing and cutting up. Coach Walker stood up and said, "I don't think I would be happy about just losing a game." The rest of the way home on the bus you could hear a pin drop. – Team Manager Bob Furches

Coach Rose was one of the best athletes I have ever seen! If it had a ball, he could play it and play it well. He would take us to Salisbury, N.C. and we would play softball, golf, putt-putt, and he was clearly the best player in all of these by a wide margin. In a way he was just one of us. Coach Walker had the unenviable task of taking over the team after Coach Rose became ill. To his credit he did not change the system. This allowed the team to continue its winning ways. Both men had a huge impact on the players lives and taught us the value of integrity, honesty and hard work. I will be forever grateful for the time we had together. – Bob Francis

I knew Coach Rose when I was younger because he played ball with my dad. He was always so good to me. I feel sure Coach Rose and Coach Walker were the reason I became a coach. I always wanted to be like them. And I wanted my players to look up to me the way I looked up to them. One of my greatest honors was to be able to coach John Rose, Coach Rose's son. He was so much like Coach Rose, and I enjoyed coaching him, seeing Gwyn and his sisters supporting him, and just knowing I was doing for John what his dad had done for me!

Coach Rose and Coach Walker were such an inspiration to each of us. They kept us positive and pushed us toward our goal. We respected them and wanted to do our very best for them. It was hard when Coach Rose got so ill, but we never lost sight of our goal because of Coach Rose and Coach Walker. – Jimmy Thompson

CHAPTER 3

THE PLAYERS

"We won because of great coaching, commitment to fundamentals and a team that supported one another on and off the court." – Terry Shatley

The 1965 Panther Championship team consisted of fourteen players. At the time of this writing in 2023, three players were deceased: David Pell Bower, Larry Cockerham and Roger Howell. In addition, a team manager, Jimmy Reeves, also passed away. May they rest in peace and may their memory be a blessing.

For this chapter of the book, players were asked to respond to specific questions. The intent is for readers to be informed, not only about the team members as players, but also as individuals. The following are some of the responses supplied by the players.

Michael Badger

Number: 24

Position: Big guard; Small forward

Bio: Father: James A. Badger – Family owner of Badger Funeral Home, West Jefferson, N.C. Mother: Erma H. Badger – Beautician and Sales Specialist. Michael graduated from UNC School of Pharmacy in 1970. Lifelong UNC Tar Heel fan; Golf as a hobby. Pharmacist in North Carolina from 1970-2021. Owner of People's Drug Store in West Jefferson.

As a high school student my dream was to be a coach in baseball, football and basketball, but my parents said there was too much politics in teaching and coaching. They were against my decision to teach and coach. In December 1959, my dad and Dr. Carson Keys bought out Graybeal's Drug Store in West Jefferson.

I began working in the snack bar on Saturdays and holidays. From there I began working in the pharmacy department and I knew then that I wanted to go to UNC Pharmacy School to become a pharmacist.

Championship Team Reflections: The 1965 Team was comprised of not only good kids, but intelligent kids, who became good, productive citizens of society. Our team players went on to work in such careers as doctors, pharmacists, coaches, teachers, architects, businessmen, engineers, telephone company workers, athletic directors and a preacher.

We had all the ingredients of a championship team: Height, ball-handlers, shooters and especially team chemistry, striving together for one single goal – to win a state championship.

Lanney Blevins

Number: 12 (Co-Captain)

Position: Guard

Bio: I have lived in Kingsport, Tennessee since June of 1969. I graduated with a B. S. in Chemical Engineering from NCSU in 1969, and worked for thirty-eight years for Eastman Chemical Company, which was part of Eastman Kodak until 1994. I retired in 2007 as Managing Director of Primestar, which was a joint venture between Eastman and Rhoda (a French-German Company). I was fortunate to travel to France and Germany several times and made a trip to South Africa for a supplier visit. I grew up in downtown Jefferson and lived across the road from the Jefferson United Methodist Church.

In 1969, I married Aleta Faye Owen. She went to Appalachian State for three years, finishing her teaching degree in 1970 at ETSU in Johnson City, TN. She also has an advanced degree in Guidance and School Management. She retired in 2011, after forty years of teaching at the high school level. My daughter, Christy, was born in 1981. She completed a degree in chemical engineering from the University of Tennessee. We have a grandson, Carter, who is eleven, and a granddaughter, Genevieve, who is eight. They both love the Jefferson Museum, and specifically the display of the 1965 Team.

Coach and Katy Walker helped me start dating Aleta. In 1966, Aleta worked as secretary for Coach Walker during her study period. I was home from college and playing table tennis with Coach, David Pell, and Dicky Bower. Mrs. Walker told me what a great gal Aleta was and that I should call her. I did make that phone call. The rest is history.

I have always been a huge sports fan. I enjoy golf, tennis, jogging, and snow and water skiing. In 1978, I qualified for the Boston Marathon and ran in Boston in 1979. I ran several 10K races and did some mini triathlons. I used to run from the Virginia state line to either Jefferson or to my father-in-law's place in Nathan's Creek.

Championship Team Reflections: We were a very close-knit team. I do not remember any friction on the team the entire year. We were good friends and had two hall of fame coaches during the '64-'65 season.

David Pell Bower (Deceased)
Number: 22 (Co-Captain)
Bio: Refer to his brother Dickie Bower's bio, which includes information on David Pell.
Dickie Bower
Number: 34

Bio: I was born in Jefferson in 1948 to Pell Bower, a sawmill owner and Margaret Bower, a registered nurse at Ashe Memorial Hospital. My older brother of nineteen months, David Pell Bower, was number 22 on the Panther's championship team. Our sister Jane Ann showed up in 1956. We were so much older than Jane Ann that there was not a lot of interaction with her until we were older. We had a wonderful growing up time. We had little, but as much as everyone else. We had rules that were followed out of respect. And we were taught to respect each other, adults and especially our teachers at school. We were encouraged to do well in school. College was an expectation for each of us. Jefferson had kids all over the place, so we had friends our age who loved to play ball – baseball, football, basketball and golf. David Pell and I did everything together! He was a bit older, bigger and stronger than I was, but not so much that I could not keep up. We fought like crazy yet loved each other like crazy too. We played sports year-round outside. For instance, we shot hoops and we were glad when the ground became frozen so the ball would bounce better in the dirt around the basket out in the field behind our home, where we played. As we got older and played little league, Mom and Dad always made sure we got a ride to practice and to games. Dad, especially, would come to many of our games. One of the sports he got us involved in was golf, which we got good at and continue playing to this day. Dad played with us on the course till he was almost eighty years of age.

Playing all those team sports taught us that you don't always win. But you continue working. Try hard. Learn from others.

After high school I attended UNC Pharmacy School, class of 1971. My years in Chapel Hill were so influential in my life. I made lifelong friends there. For example, I'm part of a group of twenty-eight guys who have been doing annual golf trips for almost fifty years. I moved to Greensboro, N.C. after graduation, and have lived there since. I worked at a retail pharmacy for forty-five years. After marriage we had twins, a boy and a girl, Jason and Erin, who were great kids. They are now raised with children of their own. My wife, Brenda, and I now have six granddaughters.

I enjoy working in the yard, cooking, golf, and all things UNC. From my mother I learned to love reading. She told me I would never be bored if I had a book in my hands. So, I learned to continually have a book to read. I also enjoy spending time with family and many friends.

Championship Team Reflections: Being a part of the '65 Team has become part of my identity. It was such a special group of guys, who liked each other and still care for one another to this day! I got to watch often from the bench as this team did its thing. I can still see my brother, David Pell, moving out on his man on the wing. I'm thinking, "This guy is in trouble now. There goes Dave!" And Dave's hands would start zipping around and many times he would steal the ball and he'd start a fastbreak down the floor, usually hitting Charlie Bowers for a layup.

It was a joy to be a part of something that was years in the making! Fun years. Fun learning with Coach Rose about things life in addition to basketball. Fun to be a team member.

Charlie Bowers (Co-Captain)

Number: 10

Position: Point Guard

Bio: I was born in Jefferson, the third of four children. My dad owned and operated the grocery store and gasoline station in East Jefferson, across from the Rancho Restaurant. I received a Mathematics degree from North Carolina State University in 1969. I am married to Nancy Cox Bowers. We have two children and three grandchildren. After teaching one year in the Raleigh area, I returned to Ashe County for a teaching career. I taught at Healing Springs Elementary School from 1970 through 1988. Following Healing Springs, I taught, coached and was athletics director at Ashe Central High School from 1989 until 1999.

Championship Team Reflections: What an awesome experience to be a part of this team! We had two great coaches to guide us. Coach Rose taught us about basketball, but even much more about living life to the fullest. He packed a lot of life into his relatively few years! I remember Coach Walker and his wife, Katy, lived in a mobile home next door to my family during my high school days. Coach Walker did a super job of taking over the team from Coach Rose.

Larry Cockerham (Deceased)

Number: 44

Position: Forward

Bio: (Submitted by Larry's Family from Larry's Point of View) – I was born in Ashe County, North Carolina in 1947 to Hazel and Jack Cockerham. I was raised on my family's farm in the mountains of Ashe. I was surrounded by many aunts, uncles and cousins while growing up. Upon graduation from Ashe Central, I went to North Carolina State University and majored in Landscape Architecture, where I received my degree. I then began to work in Raleigh, North Carolina, at an architectural firm. Later I moved to Nashville, TN., and began working at Metro Parks and Recreation, where I served as the planning superintendent for thirty years. I met Darlene Whaley while working in the same building for Metro Beautification. We married in 1980. In 1982 we were gifted with a son, Brian Cockerham. While continuing to work, I took on the role of an athlete's father, documenting most of Brian's athletic career. Brian met and married Shannon Cain in 2005, and gifted Darlene and I with a grandson, Camden in 2006, and granddaughter, Katelyn, in 2009.

Championship Team Reflections: From what I remember from my father's perspective, attending the Hall of Fame Induction Ceremony was one of his proudest moments. He had his immediate family in attendance, and we were able to see his hometown, his teammates, and spend the weekend celebrating with him.

Bob Francis (Co-Captain)

Number: 50

Position: Center

Bio: I was born in Helton, N.C. My father, Don L. Francis, was Clerk of the Superior Court in Ashe County for many years. My mother, Minnie Belle, ran The Northwest Trading Post in Glendale Springs, N.C. I grew up on a farm in Smethport, N.C., with two older brothers (Joe and Tom). We had 12,000 chickens and 30 head of dairy cattle on 88 acres of land, so we kept busy.

I transferred from West Jefferson Elementary School to Jefferson Elementary School to begin the 7th grade. At the time I thought it was a catastrophe, but it turned out that's where I met the future members of the 1965 team and Coach Rose. After high school I went to Duke University on an academic scholarship and walked-on the freshman and varsity basketball teams. I was the 6th man on the freshman team and pretty much sat at the end of the bench on the varsity.

I did have the opportunity to play under Coach Vic Bubas, who was a very positive influence. I got to practice and play with Bob Verga, Jack Marin, Mike Lewis, and a lot of other fine young men, experiencing big time college basketball firsthand. During Christmas break of my sophomore year, most of the varsity got kicked off the team for going to a party and were seen drinking alcohol. There were only six or seven players left to play and I was one of them. We beat Penn State despite our reduced numbers, and I got some action that night.

My father, Don, passed away at the beginning of my junior year, so I felt the need to go to work part time to help with expenses, which left no time for basketball. After graduating from Duke, I went to work for Lowe's Hardware, as an office manager. During this time, I had a life-changing dream. I was at my own funeral, in the casket at the front of the church and sitting in the back row. I asked the person sitting next to me, "What did this guy do with his life?" He leaned back and pointed to a Lowe's tractor-trailer that was packed full of paper and said, "He filled out all those forms!" I awoke in a cold sweat, and knew I had to change professions. I went back to Duke and took a series of aptitude and interest tests to help discern a new vocation. I was told that I should consider being a physician. It had never dawned on me before that moment that medicine was a possible career for me. I had taken almost no science courses as an undergraduate, so I had to take a lot of these courses before I could even apply for medical school.

I decided to go for it, borrowed $5,000 from a relative, and went back to school at UNC and NC State to get the science courses required. More than one advisor told me I was wasting my time, that I would never get into medical school, but I persisted and was fortunate to be admitted to Duke University Medical School. After medical school I stayed at Duke for a two-year General and Thoracic Surgery residency, a four-year Orthopedic Surgery residency, and a six-month Hand Surgery fellowship.

I knew I wanted to live in the mountains of North Carolina, so I drew a line fifty miles on each side of the Blue Ridge Parkway and decided that I would live somewhere between those two lines. I practiced Orthopedic/Hand surgery in Hendersonville, N.C., for thirty-five years, then retired. One of my previous partners asked me to come out of retirement and work at the Asheville V A Hospital, which I did for about ten years. What a privilege and honor it was to take care of those veterans!

I retired in May of 2022, and now spend my time repairing, painting, and generally improving some rental real estate that I own. I like to travel, fly fish for trout and watch Duke basketball and football games on television.

Championship Team Reflections: My most amazing memory of the 1965 basketball experience was when we came home from the tournament in Winston-Salem and the highway patrol met us at the Ashe County line and escorted us to the Rancho Drive-In. The crowd turnout was unbelievable! I heard an old man say, "I haven't seen this many people out in Ashe County since the railroad came to town!" I had trouble taking in what had happened, and that it was all over.

Roger Howell (Deceased)

Number: 54

Position: Forward

Bio: Roger died on July 29th, 2019. His funeral service was held at the Badger Funeral Home Chapel on Friday, August 2nd, 2019, at 2PM. His obituary read as follows:

Roger Gale Howell, age 72 of Crumpler died Monday, July 29th, 2019, at Forsyth Medical Center. Mr. Howell was born December 4th, 1946, in Ashe County to the late Spencer Howell and Beulah Hamm Howell. In addition to his parents, he was preceded in death by his wife, Berna Jo Ann Blevins Howell; his son, Randy Howell; brother, Earl, Eugene and Ralph Howell; and sister, Evelyn Phipps.

Roger was a member of Shelter Baptist Church. He never met a stranger and was a friend to many. Roger was a member of the N C State Championship team of Ashe Central High School. He retired from Skyline Telephone after many years of service.

He enjoyed working outside and took great pride in keeping his yard looking good. He also enjoyed spending time at Hardee's Restaurant with his friends.

Mr. Howell is survived by his granddaughter, Anna Wyatt of Lansing; brothers, Dale Howell, Ronnie Howell and Mike Howell, all of Jefferson; sisters, Geneva Phillips and Freda Hardy both of Jefferson and Hilda Brookshire of Wilkesboro. Several nieces and nephews also survive.

Pallbearers and honorary pallbearers will be members of the Ashe Central State Basketball Championship Team, Morris Walker, Charlie Bowers, Warren Witherspoon, Dickie Bower, Eddie Vannoy, David Mullis, Lanney Blevins, Jim Thompson, John Jackson and David Pell Bower.

Championship Team Reflections: A classic story is relayed about Coach Walker insisting the reluctant-to-shoot Roger would shoot perimeter jump shots during the State playoff games. Charlie Bowers passes the ball to Roger on the wing. Roger is so nervous that he flips the ball back to Charlie. Coach Walker jumps up off the bench and yells, "Roger! Shoot the ball!" Charlie throws another pass to Roger. Roger said that he looked up at the basket and it looked like the size of an aspirin, about 90 feet away. He nervously shot and the result was nothing but net! His shooting and scoring continued several times down the floor and the other team had to call a time out. Morris looked at Roger with a huge smile. Roger reflected in speaking to Morris Walker later, "Coach, I saw you looking at me with a big smile on your face. This gave me the confidence I needed."

Championship Team Reflections: In an interview with Josh Beckworth, Roger recalls: "My dad never saw me play in an Ashe Central basketball game until the end of the '65 championship season. I think the guys who gathered to chat at Harry Koontz's Service Station pressured him into attending. As we were warming up in Winston-Salem, prior to our first state tournament game, I heard a familiar voice yell out, 'Alright, boy, I want to see something!' I was shocked! It was my dad! It really meant a lot to me that he was finally there, seeing us play."

John Jackson

Number: 20

Position: Forward

Bio: I am a native Ashe Countian. My parents were educators. Dad, R. O. Jackson, was principal of Ashe Central. Mother taught at Jefferson Elementary. I taught school as well and have served as a pastor in the Primitive Baptist Church for twenty-seven years.

I was, and still am, an active outdoorsman. I own and hunt Plott Hounds on small and large game. I was president of the American Plott Association and have served on its board of directors several times. I write a great deal, contributing articles to magazines and yearbooks. These articles pertain to hounds and hunting.

Championship Team Reflections: As to the team, I scrimmaged a great deal and played occasionally. However, I was greatly honored to be a part of this squad. I have a lot of fond memories. One of these good memories that really impressed me was Coach Walker and his concern for his players. I know of instances where he gave snacks to players after games because they could not afford it. He gave money to players who came from difficult home situations as well. The lessons learned were not just basketball, but also about living life.

David W. Mullis, Jr.

Number: 42

Position: Forward

Bio: I was born in Jefferson N. C., but lived many years in Nocona, Texas. My father was from Ashe County, but my mother was born and raised in Nocona, Texas. As a family, we lived primarily in Texas where I played football and basketball. I enjoyed significant success in basketball at Nocona High, making the all-conference team during my freshman and sophomore years.

My family moved back to Ashe County during my junior year in high school. I became a starting forward on the State Championship team. I was named to the All-Northwest basketball teams during my junior and senior years.

After graduation from ACHS, I attended Appalachian State University and played for four years for Coach Bob Light on the Mountaineer basketball team. During my last quarter at ASU, I married my long-time girlfriend, Becky McNeill. I attended the University of Tennessee at Knoxville completing a Master of Science Degree. After teaching health sciences at George Wythe High School in Richmond, VA., and coaching both football and basketball, I returned to the University of Tennessee to work toward a Ph.D. degree. In August 1976, I received a Ph.D. from UT with a major in public health and collateral concentrations in human anatomy and physiology. After graduation from UT, I joined the faculty at Radford University, teaching in the health sciences program and as assistant basketball coach.

However, this was not the best career fit for me at the time. Subsequently, I accepted the executive director position with a Salem, VA based Foundation for Medical Care, working with physician peer review among Southwest Virginia hospitals. During this period, our first daughter, Megan was born. In 1981, Becky and I moved to Minneapolis, MN, where I joined Cardiac Pacemakers, Inc., an Eli Lilly owned company, developing and marketing cardiovascular products. It was during this time that our second daughter, Meredith, was born. During my 9-plus years with CPI, I served as Director of Medical Services and Regulatory Affairs and Clinical Programs, obtaining FDA approval for the first implantable cardioverter defibrillator, a series of insulin infusion devices and other novel therapeutic products. In 1989, I accepted a senior management position directing regulatory affairs and clinical programs for CR Bard, Inc., a fortune 500 company.

We relocated to the Atlanta, GA. area and I continued with Bard, working in a variety of senior management positions for 9-plus years. In 1998, I served as Vice President of Medical Affairs for London International Group for two years. After that, I started my own consulting company (Mullis & Associates, Inc.) providing regulatory affairs and clinical trials support services for pharmaceutical companies, biotech firms and medical device companies. In 2004, I accepted a position with the University of Georgia College of Pharmacy as Director of International Biomedical Regulatory Sciences developing a graduate degree education program, while continuing directing operations at my consulting company. I retired from UGA in 2020 as Professor Emeritus in the College of Pharmacy.

I continue to be moderately active in Mullis & Associates, Inc. My community service includes the City of Good Hope city council, and I am Vice Mayor for the city. I am an active member of Emmanuel Episcopal Church in Athens, GA.

Championship Team Reflections: The team rapport was unbelievable! Although I had known many of the team members since middle school, I had not been a member of the squad until my junior year. Coach Rose welcomed me to the team when I returned to Ashe County, and he prepared the team members to accept me as a player. As Coach Rose's health continued to decline, Coach Walker assumed the leadership role. Yet he always referred to the team as Wade's team. The leadership and humility that Coach Walker demonstrated was something that I appreciated both at the time and in the years that followed.

Terry Shatley

Number: 52

Position: Guard, Forward

Bio: I was born in Ashe County. My father, Guy Shatley, was an insurance agent. My mother was a housewife. I have three sisters, Janet, who is deceased, Tammie, and Bonnie. I have worked in many aspects of construction and at Lowe's Home Improvement in Durham, N.C.

I love to hunt and fish but am unable to do so due to health issues. I've always loved sports. I started baseball as a youngster, then played pony league, and some beyond that level. I was a pitcher and had good luck with that position. My pitching repertoire included a curve ball that broke down and out, and a fast ball. I wanted to play football, but my mom wouldn't let me because of a possible injury. I feel I was a good basketball player, but not an excellent one. I just enjoyed being on a super team.

Championship Team Reflections: We won because of a commitment to the fundamentals of basketball and a team that "clicked" on and off the court. Being part of this team taught me a lot about life. I later learned to incorporate the fundamentals of Christ-following faith into my life. Basics such as prayer, scripture reading and sharing life with others have been ways I have discovered to be sustained and to grow in faith formation.

Jimmy Thompson

Number: 14

Position: Forward

Bio: I was born in Jefferson and raised in Laurel Springs. I am the only son of Venner and Barbara Thompson. I attended Nathans Creek Elementary School, Ashe Central High School, Lees-McRae Junior College, and Appalachian State University. I taught at Riverview for two years, Nathans Creek for two years, and then moved to Ashe Central High School until my retirement. I taught Health, Physical Education, and weight training. I started my coaching career with the Jefferson Braves Little League Team when I was eighteen. I was assistant baseball coach at Ashe Central High School while teaching at Nathans Creek.

At ACHS I coached varsity basketball, boys and girls, varsity baseball, varsity girls' softball, slow pitch and fast pitch. I was also an assistant coach in football. I played baseball and softball from the time I was nine years old until I was sixty-three. I played with an over-fifty softball team out of Raleigh, NC, and we won many national and world tournaments.

My hobby now is reloading and attending rifle shooting tournaments.

My wife Alice and I have been married fifty-four years and we have two sons, Jimmy, Jr. and Andrew. I was able to coach both my sons all through high school. Jimmy, Jr. and Charlotte have two sons, Grant and Wesley. Grant played football at Lenoir-Rhyne and Wesley is playing currently at Wingate. I gladly helped Jimmy, Jr. coach both boys in Junior League basketball and Little League baseball. Andrew lives in Kernersville and has a son, Evan, and a daughter, Toni. Evan wrestled last year, and Toni is on the golf team.

Championship Team Reflections: The fellowship of this team was amazing! No one was selfish or only focused upon themselves. It was an honor to be a part of such a great team. This group will forever remain friends, and we all miss the ones we have lost. This team was so special because we were coached by the best, and they would not accept anything less.

I loved watching our starting five dominate. Watching Charlie take charges and sliding across the floor was a hoot! He did it so well. We always had a great time going to and from the games. Of course, it is easy to be happy when you are winning!

Eddie Vannoy

Number: 30

Position: Point Guard

Bio: I was born and raised in Ashe County, NC, to Jim and Wilma Vannoy, along with two brothers, Mark and Tim. My dad started James R. Vannoy & Sons Construction Company in 1952. I started working alongside him in 1971. I am still actively working in our Jefferson office. My hobbies and interests include collecting cars and playing golf.

Championship Team Reflections: I am very proud to have been a part of the 1965 State Championship Team. To my knowledge, this is the only team to have won a State Championship from Ashe County. This is something I have carried with me and been able to tell this narrative my entire life. This experience taught me that no matter what you do in life, you need to work hard and be a team member. I made a lot of friends for life on this team, and it taught me that you never give up when it comes to the things you wish to achieve.

Warren Witherspoon

Number: 54

Position: Forward

Bio: I was born and raised, along with my three sisters, in Ashe County, North Carolina. My parents were William and Louise Witherspoon. In March of 1968, I married Barbara Arnold. We have been married for fifty-five years. I have a daughter, Amber, and a son-in-law, T.J. Murphy. I also have two wonderful grandchildren: Talon and Piper.

I spent two years in the military, the last year of which was in Vietnam. I served in the U.S. Army, 173rd Airborne. I came home from Vietnam unscathed except for my exposure to agent orange, which years later would cause me to have prostate cancer and kidney disease. I worked in the grocery industry for Lowe's Foods as a store manager for ten years. I was also a district manager for 3D Supermarket for two years. The rest of my career was spent with Frito-Lay, for thirty years as a route salesman. I retired at age sixty-one.

My interests include traveling to Disney World with my family. I have visited Disney World forty-five times. My favorite hobbies are bass fishing and spending time with my grandkids.

Championship Team Reflections: I was very happy for the team. I was not able to dress out for the state tournament due to a severe leg injury. However, the coaches insisted that I remain on the team as one of the players. They included me in events that followed winning the championship. I think that tells you a lot about the quality of the team. No one was left out!

1965 Championship Team

JEFFERSON, N. C.

Coach - Morris H. Walker

Manager - Jimmy Reeves

Team Nickname - Panthers

School Colors - Black and White

Players	Jersey No. White	Jersey No. Black	Height	Weight	Age	Class
David Pell Bower	22	23	5' 10"	145	17	12
Dickie Bower	34	33	5' 10"	145	16	11
Bob Francis	50	51	6' 6"	192	18	12
Charlie Bowers	10	11	5' 10"	145	17	12
Lanney Blevins	12	13	5' 10"	145	18	12
Roger Howell	54	53	6' 4"	198	18	12
David Mullis	42	43	6' 5"	192	16	11
Larry Cockerham	44	45	6' 2"	205	17	12
Mike Badger	24	25	6' 2"	190	17	12
John Jackson	20	21	6' 0"	147	17	11
Jimmy Thompson	14	15	6' 0"	150	17	11
Eddie Vannoy	30	31	5' 7"	145	16	11
Terry Shatley	52	41	5' 10"	140	16	11

Team Record: Won 22 Lost 1

Leading Scorers: Bob Francis - 452 points - Charlie Bowers - 304 points

David Mullis - 304 points

ACHS Team Roster

"Gone, but not forgotten."

CHAPTER 4

THE SUPPORT

"Our school was our main support, from the principal to the custodians. Everyone, whether student or teacher, was there to cheer us on. Our families were our biggest cheerleaders. Then as the year and season progressed, the entire county came together and supported us all the way to the state championship!" – Jimmy Thompson

I have heard it said, "It takes a village to raise a child." Perhaps it could also be accurately stated that it takes a county to raise a championship team. The Panthers were fortunate to have received widespread and strong support from Ashe County and beyond. Some of this support is listed in this chapter.

THE SCHOOL

John Jackson reminisces, "Students at Ashe Central sent a lengthy telegram of support to the team while in Winston-Salem. Nearly every student and teachers' names were listed on it!"

Excitement was in the air at ACHS! A regular season record of nineteen wins against only one loss had provided a lot of momentum and was cause for great celebration. The home gymnasium was packed for each game. Very often conversation in the school hallways was pertaining to the Panthers success. How far would this team go? How deep into the post-season would they make it?

Then, when the team won the district tournament, the conversation and confidence only grew! When Central entered the state tournament many students and their families, along with others, traveled to Winston-Salem to support the squad. ACHS also took activity buses. Students, teachers and faculty alike were promoting and parading their Panther pride.

The ACHS Gym where the Panthers played their home games.

THE FANS

Winston-Salem Journal Sports Editor, Garland Smith, in the March 19, 1965, issue penned the following in an article titled, ASHE CENTRAL WINS CLASS 2A STATE CHAMPIONSHIP:

"Who was responsible for this winning team? I will be the first to say it was a four-way combination. First, their beloved and now late Coach Wade Rose, who passed away on Monday from cancer, less than 30 hours after their victory. The Ashe Central team. I say without pause this is, and was, one of the best coordinated and cooperative teams found anywhere this season. Coach Morris Walker, who led the boys when more than just another basketball game faced them. And last, but not least, the faithful sports fans of Ashe County, who drove many miles to support their winning team that boasted a 25 and 1 record after Saturday night's State Championship."

Garland Smith's colleague and long-time respected sportswriter, Mary Garber wrote, in her Journal article with the headline, A SURE SIGN OF SUCCESS: TURNAWAY CROWD AT FINALS:

"Ashe Central and Anson County did something no other 2-A teams have done. They had a turn away crowd for the finals of the state 2-A tournament at Reynolds gym Saturday night.

Tournament manager Herman Bryson had to stop selling tickets because there just wasn't another inch of space in the gym. Even so, many fans had to stand up all during the game because there were no seats left. The kids made the best of it. They got to sit on the floor.

At the beginning of the state playoffs, tournament officials had marked off and designated four distinct sections in the gym bleachers for the four participating teams' fans. As the tournament advanced it was clear that Ashe County fans had a much higher turnout than the other three schools. So, the officials changed course. They marked off two bleacher sections, an entire side, for the Panther fans due to their overwhelming support.

The 1965 tournament was probably the best attended of any since the 2-A Tournament came to Winston-Salem. There was a full house every night even before the "no vacancy" of Saturday. And it's hard to estimate how many people drove by Reynolds gym, saw the mob and decided to pass on by."

In Reynold's Gym, it was standing room only. The parking lot was full to over-flowing. Ashe County Sheriff, Gene Bare, was anxious to see the state tournament game as well. Gene drove a County Sheriff's car to Winston. When he could find no parking, and the game was about to commence, he decided to park at the front entrance. As the game was ready to get underway, an announcement came over the gym P A system, "Would the driver of the Ashe County Sheriff's car, please move this vehicle parked at the entrance of the gym!" Sheriff Bare embarrassingly had to walk out in front of all the fans, to move the car. It was an awkward moment for Bare and for the Ashe County fans. Yet, after the game, and for years, this account provided legendary levity.

Ashe County fans were both many and faithful in attendance at the state tournament. As Central kept advancing and the prospect of winning the championship was becoming more and more, not only a possibility, but a probability, even more excitement was generated. 1965 ACHS student, Becky McNeill Mullis shares, "I was a library assistant for Mrs. Katy Walker, Coach Walker's wife, during my high school years. I loved to draw and paint so most of my library time was spent making bulletin boards or posters for the library and the school. As our basketball team progressed through the tournament to the final game, we just knew we were going to win! Katy asked me to create a banner for that anticipated win. She and I discussed what the banner should look like and what it should say. We decided it should be big since this would be a BIG win for our team.

The final design featured a large panther, our school mascot, and the words, "We're It – State Champions That Is". I completed the banner the day before the team and fans were to leave for the Big Game, the final game of the tournament. I did not see the banner again until after the tournament when it was displayed at the entrance to the gymnasium at Ashe Central High School."

The Ashe Central Championship Banner

Legend has it that one of the ACHS teachers, Mr. Paul Shatley, folded this banner and placed it inside his jacket. Near the end of the game with Anson County, when the Panthers were assured of the win, he took the banner out, and proudly displayed it on the gym wall!

Becky continues, "The championship year was an exciting time for the entire ACHS student body. Growing up in North Carolina, basketball was a popular sport. We had a feeling that this was going to be a special year for the team. Coach Rose and Coach Walker encouraged everyone to get behind the team and cheer them on. As the basketball season progressed, and the team kept winning, we became even more excited. We started to believe that we could make it to the state tournament, maybe even win! We attended as many games as we could during the season. We had regular "pep rallies" to boost team and school spirit. Everyone was involved!

During the state tournament, many of us were able to attend the games to cheer on the team. I think all the cars and trucks leaving Ashe County for Winston-Salem were full of ACHS students and other fans. We were so excited that our section of the tournament gym was packed with Central fans.

At the same time, we knew that Coach Rose was gravely ill. So, we were all praying for him as we continued to cheer on our team. We remembered his leadership of the team and hoped he would be able to realize his team had won the state championship. His wife, Gwen, later let us know that he knew the team had won before he lapsed into a final coma.

Upon this team's return to Ashe County, people from all over the county were at the Rancho Drive-In, our ACHS hangout, to greet the team. I remember it was a time when the whole county, even the other rival county high schools, were proud of what this team had accomplished."

Fan, Jackie Reeves Badger, a fifth grader at Nathan's Creek Elementary School in 1965, recollects, "I talked my dad and mom into taking me all three nights to Winston-Salem at the state tournament site. I sat right behind the ACHS cheerleaders and yelled out of my Pepsi-Cola cup to make my voice louder! I later became a student and cheerleader at Ashe Central. And I still have that Pepsi cup. Once a Panther always a Panther!"

THE CHEERLEADERS

Maureen Shoaf Blackburn was a member of the 1965 Cheerleading Squad. Following are some of her memories of the championship team.

"When I was a student at Jefferson Elementary School in Jefferson, N.C., a new teacher appeared on the scene. He was tall and lanky, soft-spoken and friendly. The students took to him immediately. His name was Wade Rose. Besides being a teacher, he was the boys' and girls' basketball coach. Although I was not a student in his class, I was on the girls' basketball team.

One afternoon Coach Rose had all the players assembled on the bleachers to discuss some points he wanted to go over. Some of my friends and I had heard something funny and could not stop laughing. The harder we tried to stop, the harder we laughed. Coach Rose was not amused. He put up with it as long as he could. In his usual quiet manner, he asked if we would like to share with everyone what we found so funny. Being thoroughly embarrassed, we sheepishly declined. We did appreciate his low-key way of shutting us up.

When I was a junior at Ashe Central High School, I was on the varsity cheerleading squad. We were always up for the games because our boys played so well, like a well-oiled machine. Some of these boys had played together for six years. Every game was exciting. I really enjoyed helping lead the fans in cheers for the team.

When we had an away game outside the county, we often boarded the bus at the Rancho, a small restaurant in East Jefferson. On one such occasion, I was paying for my burger and fries and noticed Coach Rose sitting in a booth directly across the aisle from me. He was eating a hot dog. Much to my surprise, he had lettuce and tomato on his hot dog! Certainly not the usual fare. I'm sure I made some comments, but thankfully I cannot remember what they were.

As the season wore on our boys got better and better. I have forgotten when Coach Rose learned of his cancer and had to stop coaching, but whenever it was, our guys just played all the harder and better to show Coach Rose their love for him.

On the afternoon of one of the post-season tournament games, the team and the cheerleaders went by Coach Rose's home to give and to receive pep talks. He was barely able to stand to greet us but stand he did! I could not help noticing that his clothes hung on his frail body like on a coat hanger. I still have that image in my mind's eye today. I knew in my heart of hearts we were going to win! I felt assured that the boys would give their all to win for the beloved coach. With heavy hearts we got on the bus and headed down the mountain for the game.

The state tournament championship game was filled with excitement in the air! Being cheerleaders, we had front row seats and could see all the action up close! Our guys were hitting shots. It seemed they couldn't miss. They were hitting many shots from where the three-point line is now. The stands were filled with Ashe Central fans, as well as other folks from the county, who came to cheer on our mountain team.

What a victory it was for the team, the fans, and most of all for Coach Rose. He lived just long enough to know we won the state championship! His hard work had paid off. His race was won. The celebration at school the next week was bittersweet, jubilant and sorrowful. We had won the victory but lost our beloved coach. He was such a fine man, revered by students and faculty alike. He accomplished greatness through his calm, loving nature. We still miss him. He was the best."

Another Panther cheerleader, Libby Sheets Hoffman remembers, "During the '64-'65 school year I was captain of the varsity cheerleaders. The squad included: Sue McMillan, Margo Sheets, Maureen Shoaf, Cindy McNeil, Marshall Stanley, Ann Bare and Carolyn Watson.

The basketball team just kept winning, game after game. As both a cheerleader and a student, it was a magical year. The mood at school was upbeat, positive and encouraging. Everyone seemed to feel a part of something BIG. Pep rallies were loud with lots of student participation. Games were filled with fans whether home or away.

Playing in the state playoffs was something no other Ashe County team had done up until that time. We were so excited! Going to Winston-Salem and staying in a hotel was a first for me. I had never done that before. I shared a room with two other cheerleaders, and Sara Lewis, who was the team scorekeeper. Almost immediately, someone in our room spilled a box of loose powder on the carpet. I panicked and wondered if we girls would have to pay for a new carpet. Our sponsor, Katy Walker, calmed us by reassuring us that it could be vacuumed and all would be well.

The first night of the playoffs the gym was packed. As I cheered, I noticed there were players and students from Beaver Creek, and other schools, supporting our team. I did not expect this. After all, we were rivals. It seemed the county had united around our team. The second game saw the very same – same support, same results. We won! We were going to the championship game. We were on cloud nine. Only one more game, the championship!

The next night even more people were there from Ashe County! I was both a bundle of nerves and the happiest person on earth. We were playing the most important game ever! We heard that Coach Rose had taken a turn for the worse. He was on our minds, and we really wanted this game for him. The boys did what they had done all season – THEY WON! And we were ecstatic!"

ACHS teacher Mary June Sheets, older sister to cheerleaders Libby and Margo, assisted Katy Walker, who was the cheerleaders sponsor during the '64-'65 season. 'During the state tournament, Katy and I took the cheerleaders shopping in Winston-Salem. And we would take them out to eat while staying in Winston for the tournament,' shares Mary June. 'It was a very exciting time for our school and for our county. I was grateful to be associated with the 1965 Team and to help Katy with sponsoring the Central cheerleaders.'

The next morning, we got on the activity bus to head home to Ashe County. Coach Walker got on the bus and told us that Coach Rose was not doing well at all. The ride home was rather somber. When we arrived at East Jefferson, at the Rancho, a big crowd was waiting and cheering and welcoming us home.

The next day at school students were filled with mixed emotions. We were elated and sad at the same time. I remember Coach Rose's wife, Gwen, telling us that Coach knew about the win and that she was sure he would want us to celebrate and enjoy the victory. As a cheerleader I felt like I imagined a groupie must feel about a rock star. The 1965 ACHS Basketball Team was my rock star!"

The ACHS 1965 Cheerleader Squad

COUNTY SUPPORT

As has been mentioned multiple times, the '65 Team was supported, not only by Ashe Central fans, but by people from all around Ashe County. It was like siblings. Siblings, in sibling rivalries, and cross county high school rival teams, may fight one another, but if someone outside the family, or, in this case, outside the county, tries to pick a fight, we all stick together! After all, mountain folk have a history of sticking together.

ACHS rival player and former Beaver Creek High School coach, Marc Payne, from Beaver Creek High School writes, "I remember riding to the 1965 State 2A Championship game with Blaine Cox. Blaine later became Charlie Bowers' – ACHS's point guard – father-in-law. Blaine was a friend of my dad, Max Payne, and he offered to take me with him to the game. I jumped at the chance to go.

The game was very special and the circumstances surrounding the game were amazing. Ashe County citizens have adopted the team and its coaches as a big part of Ashe County's sports history. In fact, the '65 Championship is probably the number one sports event in Ashe County history."

Ashe County educator, coach, and administrator, Bradley McNeil reflects: "Having played at Lansing I knew and played against most of the Ashe Central players. Although we were previous competitors, I pulled for them like crazy in the state tournament. I knew they were very talented and were well coached. I knew Wade Rose from playing ball with him in the summers of my junior and senior years in school at Lansing. Also, I knew Morris and his very capable abilities as a player and coach.

During their championship run the excitement reached far outside Ashe County. Everywhere I went people found out I was from Ashe and the team was mentioned. I think not only was it a good local team, but it drew attention because of the coach's illness. The folks just wanted them to win. At Lees-McRae, where I was a student, we had a group of friends that discussed the tournament daily. When they played, we would stay up at night and listen to the radio for the score. The tournament became the main topic of discussion for the next few days. It was gratifying to me that they talked about Wade's illness and Morris' coaching all during the tournament. After the final game the excitement was there but it took a back seat with Coach Rose's death. The statement many made was, 'I'm glad he lived to know the team won!'

The team was, and still is, talked about very often. I am proud to say I helped start the Ashe County Hall of Fame and helped select the 1965 Panthers as one of the first members. The plaque is in the Hall of Fame Room at the Old Court House in Jefferson."

COMPETITORS' SUPPORT

When Coach Rose was hospitalized in the Intensive Care Unit at Baptist Hospital in Winston-Salem, N.C., Elkin High School's head boys' basketball coach, Jack Jenson visited Wade. They were intense rivals on the basketball court, but they deeply respected one another. Jack's hospital visit evidenced this regard and care for one another. In addition, Coach Jenson's wife, a registered nurse at Baptist Hospital, helped to look after Coach Rose as an in-patient.

Later, at Coach Rose's funeral in Glendale Springs, the entire West Wilkes High School team of players, along with their coach, attended the Service of Death and Resurrection. What a wonderful show of athletic conference solidarity and support! Several members of other teams were also in attendance that day.

SUPPORT STAFF

When something of significance occurs, such as participating in a state championship, for example, a lot of people work behind the scenes, enabling success. Ashe Central High School's team was no exception to this collaboration rule. Team manager Bob Furches attended to details like fresh water and clean towels on the bench. Scorekeeper Sarah Lewis Blevins recorded the numbers. Volunteer Clayborn Sheets filmed the games. And teacher Richard Blackburn drove the team bus.

Blackburn, now a retired educator and school administrator from the Ashe County School System relates:

"I have had the opportunity to work with young folks in various capacities. One of the highlights of my experiences was to be associated with the 1965 Ashe Central High School basketball team. As a teacher at Ashe Central at that time, I had many of the team members enrolled in my classes. Throughout the regular season, I served as the operator of the time clock for home games and drove the activity bus to away games. Then, because of the illness of Coach Wade Rose, I accompanied the team to the North Carolina 2-A State Tournament in Winston-Salem, North Carolina as the bus driver and assisted with logistics. In these various roles, I had an up-close view of the excitement that the team generated.

As I reflect on the '65 Team, I was impressed by the character of the team members, their concern for academics, and their passionate heart for basketball and for winning. They were motivated, disciplined, committed and optimistic. Each team member realized that there is no "I" in the word team. They were coachable and willing to accept feedback and constructive criticism.

The team had the ability to survive under stress and pressure. Each team member possessed natural leadership which gave each the ability to make quick decisions in the heat of competition. In summary, each team member had a "fire in the belly" to compete and win.

The support for the team was awesome! Not only Ashe Central but all of Ashe County was behind the team as they were victorious in the tournament. Droves of Ashe County fans attended the tournament in Winston-Salem. Upon returning to Ashe County after the victory, the bus received a police escort at the county line at Glendale Springs to the Rancho Restaurant, which was located where the Corner Store now stands. A sea of Ashe County fans awaited the team's arrival and greeted them with thunderous applause as they exited the bus."

Some memories from team scorekeeper, Sara Lewis Blevins, follow, "As scorekeeper for the ACHS basketball team, I travelled with the team to away games. As the girls were required to sit in the front of the bus, sometimes I would be in the seat located directly behind the activity bus steps. At that time Coach Rose would frequently ride while standing on the steps. Since we would often be travelling late at night, returning from games, I sometimes would nod off and bump my head on the window. Coach Rose found this amusing. I would wake up very embarrassed!

Overall, my memories of my time as scorekeeper are fond ones. I was privileged to be a part of this very special group of players, cheerleaders, managers, and especially Coaches Rose and Walker, most of whom I had attended grade school with at Jefferson Elementary School.

Following the severe illness of Coach Rose, Coach Walker took the helm and did a fantastic job! As I sat next to Coach Walker on the sidelines during the championship games, I saw that the players were led by a calm, competent champion. Following the state championship game, as we rode the bus home to Ashe County, it was both great and astounding to see so many county people, many from rival teams, giving us a grand reception as we rolled into East Jefferson on that memorable Sunday morning!"

LOCAL PROPRIETORS

Many Ashe businesses and local proprietors showed support for the championship team. Lanney Blevins recalls, "Bobby Walker, owner of The BoJo Restaurant, promised he would give us steaks if we won the state. He closed the BoJo one night and fed us T-Bone Steaks with all the trimmings. It was the first time that I had a steak, other than a hamburger steak, in a restaurant."

Michael Badger reflecting upon this same food topic relates, "Our team was treated to so many steak dinners that I think we were all tired of eating steak, if that's possible." Restaurant owners and others were seeking to express their pride in, and their appreciation for, the Ashe County team that had represented their mountain community so well. The Rancho Restaurant in East Jefferson, owned and operated by Dallas and Ginny Williams, also fed the players. In fact, when the championship Panthers returned home to Ashe County, the Rancho was the celebration venue. As the team players exited the bus, hundreds of supporters were there to welcome them home.

Support for the Panthers came from many people, from many places. There existed a two-way street of appreciation. The Central Team appreciated the help and support from all of Ashe County. And the county was grateful to have a home team make, and ultimately win, the state tournament.

Chapter 5

THE ODDS AND OBSTACLES

I think the biggest tournament obstacle we had to overcome was our nervousness about playing the bigger schools from "off the mountain." We all knew we had the ability to compete against most any team, but we had to get it right in our minds and simply play our game. – Player David Mullis

Even under the best of circumstances, putting together any sports team, and keeping the team together, is a tough task for any coach. There are so many tests and tasks in a season. There are many moving parts to monitor – the schedule, the conditioning, the coaches' aptitude, the players' attitude, etc. The following is a partial, not exhaustive, list of the challenges faced by all teams universally, including the 1965 Ashe Central High School basketball squad.

STAYING FOCUSED

There are a multitude of distractions for players, especially those of adolescent, high school age. Physiologically, teenagers are prone to be greatly influenced and impacted by their hormones, to say the very least. Emotionally, it can be a rocky season of life. And mentally, brains typically are not fully developed until the early twenties. Their bodies are growing and changing. Emotions are frequently erratic. It can be difficult to stay focused on the task at hand, much less to consistently concentrate on a long-term vision and a season goal.

This lack of staying focused and straying from the intentional path can happen to the best of us. And the '65 Panthers were no exception. The boys had their mischievous moments and devious detours. Player Lanney Blevins in a statement of total transparency confesses, "Bob, David Pell, and I got in deep trouble after the East Wilkes game. It was warm for February in Ashe County and for some reason we did not have school on Friday. We had easily beaten East Wilkes at their place. So, Bob, David Pell, and I decided to play some golf on Friday afternoon before the game. We did not play well but managed to win the game. The coaches found out later and we were in trouble. We got to run a lot of laps for that mishap and mischievous mess up.

Amid this adolescent, erratic, sometimes rocky phase, youth often have many activities to balance at the same time – family and friends, academics, other extracurricular activities, part time employment, etc. – making it hard, for instance, to specialize in one sport to the extent that it is necessary to be highly competitive, especially to the elevated level of winning a state championship. Keeping players centered upon season goals and a bold vision can easily get interrupted and side-tracked even if only one team member strays from the prescribed path toward athletic success.

Coach Rose had captured and communicated a long-term vision for a group of guys whom he would mentor, tutor and bring together as a single, supportive unit. He would develop them as individuals and collectively as a team. He envisioned a squad who would regularly be taught basketball fundamentals. And he promoted a system and a vision that would, hopefully, one day be caught and bought by all the players. To instill, and sustain, the focus and concentration needed for a bold, ambitious vision in fourteen teenagers was both a monumental and an admirable undertaking!

DEVELOPING AND MAINTAINING UNITY

Seasons can be long in duration. The energy and effort required of being a team member can be taxing and tiring. Competing against a fellow teammate for playing time can create relational conflict and jealousy. Tempers can flair. Emotions may get out of hand and, if so, the negative impact may breed dissention within the squad. Maybe there exists team toxicity. Possibly poisonous interactions amidst the players. Team meetings and regular relationship check-ins are mandatory to preserve peace and maintain togetherness.

When players place the total team mentality above the "me mentality," that is a formula for genuine harmony for the squad. The '65 Panthers evidenced this unity and harmony. The words of player John Jackson reflects their unity, "State athletic regulations required that only a set number of players per team could dress out. That required one of Ashe Central's players to sit on the bench in street clothes. Eddie Vannoy sat out during the Steadman game, Terry Shatley sat during the game with Havelock, and I had to sit during the Anson game. I didn't get to play in the championship game. But I understood why, and I held no grudges or ill feelings."

Another team player, Warren Witherspoon reflects, "I remember being injured with ligament tears in my right leg. I started to quit the team because of my injury, but Coach Rose and Coach Walker talked me out of quitting." This retention and inclusion of an injured team member is indicative of the unity and respect that was a part of the fabric and the persona of the 1965 Team. As has been stated, "A team is as good as its weakest player." A great team cares for and looks after one another. No one is left out or left behind.

From nature comes a team lesson from two kinds of birds, geese and gulls. Seagulls will attack one another, especially if another gull has some sort of perceived difference or advantage. They can often be observed dive-bombing at one another, many times picking on the weakest, most vulnerable gull. Geese, on the other hand, are known to arrange their flight patterns to include and assist their weakest members. In their classic V-pattern, the strongest geese are out in front, leading the way, providing a draft and guidance for the weaker geese.

Considering this ornithology analogy, the Panthers exemplified a team unity and respect for one another which reflected team-oriented geese, instead of individual-first gulls. Doing battle with our self-centered human nature, and our culture of extreme individualism, is a frequent and difficult obstacle to overcome. However, when a team engages in first-class acts of inclusion, such as keeping injured players on the team for the season and post-season, this is evidence of team unity. When the state playoffs limit each team to dress out only twelve players and there are fourteen players on the team, the unified team rotates squad members so that all may participate in the state tournament. These are examples of team unity overcoming selfish individualism.

PHYSICAL CONDITIONING

Staying well-conditioned physically over the course of a season can present an obstacle for a team. There is required extra energy exerted. Very seldom does a coach hear from players, "Coach, please let us run more wind sprints." Or "Coach, we especially love those suicide drills you make us run in practice." Human nature resists intensive physical workouts. We often choose the easy path. Unfortunately, when it comes to neglecting physical conditioning and choosing the path of least resistance, individual players and the team will not reach their potential. Optimal conditioning does not occur through osmosis. And it is likely opponents in superior physical shape will prevail especially in close contests. The squad that is in peak condition will often win a contest toward the last portion, in the final minutes, of a game.

After Coach Rose was unable to be on the bench and Coach Walker was taking over the reins, one of the ACHS players was asked, "What did Walker emphasize?" He responded, "As we moved toward the end of the regular season and potential post-regular-season games, Coach Walker made sure we were in tip-top condition. He really kept us in game shape."

In keeping with this conditioning theme, Bob Furches, one of the team managers on the championship team, recalls, "One thing that stands out for me is how Coach Walker got the nickname "Clyde." In 1965 some of the players had small transistor radios. We were in the locker room one afternoon after practice and one of the players turned on their radio and the song, "Ahab the Arab," by Ray Stevens came on. It included the lyrics, 'Get on your camel and ride, Clyde." One of the teammates said, 'Boy, Clyde (referring to Coach Walker) rode us hard in practice today.' The nickname stuck and from that day forward Coach was referred to as Clyde."

Keeping the team in shape was a top priority for Coach Walker. Walker knew from his years as a basketball player the importance of strength and stamina, especially regarding fourth quarter performance. During his playing years at Lansing High School, Morris learned well from Coach Charlie Stancil the critical importance of physical conditioning. The lesson paid huge and long-term dividends.

FUNDAMENTALS

Dribbling drills. Defensive slides. Layups. Bounce passes. Chest passes. Jump shots. Running offense patterns over and over. Fast break drills. Station drills. Rebound and box out practice. Man-to-man defensive principles. These are just a few of the basics of basketball. This is just a small sampling of what are known as b-ball fundamentals. Fundamentals regularly practiced form the foundation of a formable player and of a fruitful team. Faithfully and regularly rehearsing the fundamentals is a never-ending necessary habit for all players, seasoned and unseasoned alike. Not including and implementing fundamentals consistently in practice is a major roadblock, and obstacle, to a team's success.

I recall watching the great, and at the time, veteran NBA player, Michael Jordan during warmups prior to a game. He had a focused and intentional warmup routine. While many of the other players during pre-game warmups were talking and basically goofing off, Jordan remained concentrated on his shooting, even shooting layups! I thought, "One of the best players in the world, playing years and years of ball, with tremendous success, and still working on his layup shots, just like the 7th and 8th grade team." Fundamentals are essential for optimal playing performance.

Player Dickie Bower shares, "I remember Coach Rose making us learn to shoot layups left-handed. Over and over, we did this. I wondered why at the time. But over time it paid off. If you go to the basket from the left side, you use your left hand. It was the correct thing to do. It protects the ball from the defense." Yes, fundamentals ARE essential for optimal playing performance.

Coach Wade Rose insisted the team regularly practice fundamentals. John Jackson recalls, "Coach Rose was a stickler for fundamentals. Once when he attended a Wake Forest basketball game, he was so impressed with Wake's defense that he taught us the same fundamental guarding technique." Wade Rose carried a small red notebook with him. Many team-related notes are found there, including a section dedicated to the practice of basketball drills and fundamentals which he utilized for the team. Once again, quoting Jackson, "One of my takeaways from our '65 Team, take a smart, hard-working group of players, well coached, and they will beat a team of hotshots every time. Discipline and fundamentals have much to do with it!"

DISCIPLINE

For a team to be championship caliber there must be discipline. Discipline is required for instance, for eating an appropriate and healthy diet to aid in performance. Earlier from Coach Rose's red notebook we saw some dietary recommendations for players on game day. Also, there is the discipline of regular and rigorous physical conditioning in order to compete. Coach Walker ensured the team was in shape, including stamina through the fourth quarter.

Practicing fundamentals is another necessary discipline. Coach Rose drilled the team on basketball basics from the seventh grade through the twelfth grade. There is required the discipline of running team offensive and defensive sets until they become like second nature to the players, everyone playing their position and part, so that the plays are executed like a well-oiled machine. Discipline – physical, emotional and mental – is central to any successful team. Good, competent coaches demand and ensure team discipline both on and off the court.

Tom Landry, the late, great coach of the Dallas Cowboys, on one occasion was asked by a reporter, "Coach, what is the most difficult part of your job?" Landry did not hesitate in responding. "The hardest part of my job," he stated, "is making a group of grown men do what they least want to do so that they may attain what they most want in football." Coach Landry was referring to the sacrifice and self-discipline that is required of these men – strenuous workouts, healthy, self-denying habits, giving up some personal desires, etc. – so that they would have a better chance of winning a Super Bowl ring.

Coach Rose ran disciplined and orderly practices with the Panther players. Charlie Bowers informs, "Coach Rose was a stickler for taped ankles for each of us players. Our ankles were taped for every practice and for every game. Next, we came out on the gym floor and did "tip toes" drill, which served to strengthen our ankles and feet. Then we did a series of offensive and defensive drills. This was followed by 3-on-3 and 5-on-5 game simulations. We would finish our practices each day with shooting free throws." There was guidance and intentionality even with practice sessions.

Team discipline and self-denial pose obstacles and roadblocks to overcome. The temptation is great for individual players to go their own way and do their own thing. The pull is strong to quit the hard work. Many take the easy way out. Yet, to those who remain disciplined and work hard on their game and seek to help the team, the effort can pay great rewards.

THE CHALLENGE OF CHEMISTRY

Yet another barrier to battle when it comes to developing a team is the sometimes very difficult task of gaining good chemistry amongst team players. A high school coach does not typically have the luxury of recruiting players. Usually, the school district in which student-players reside determines the school at which they play. In other words, from a public school's coach's perspective you get the hand you are dealt. The personnel you pick from to form your roster is limited to the school's student enrollment. Sometimes, through the luck of the draw, a new player moves into the school district and makes an immediate positive impact, perhaps filling a position gap for the team.

A portion of ideal chemistry for a basketball squad includes having a good balance of inside, or frontcourt players, as well as backcourt participants. Having the right combination and numbers of guards, forwards and centers is typically critical for a championship team. The team needs strong post players, efficient guards, and accurate shooting wing forwards and guards. When a high school team can place on the court what is called in basketball terminology, a solid number one, or point guard, who directs the team both verbally and with their play, who can penetrate the defense and provide assists to other players, the foundation for success is laid. Next, if this same team can build on this foundation by developing strong shooters through a number two shooting guard and a number three, small shooting forward, the outside offense is set and will be formable. Then for the final pieces of the position puzzle, a powerful post presence is necessary through the four and five positions, power forward and center. When all five positions are in place, and those respective players are strong in performing their respective roles, a viable nucleus is formed.

However, a team is not complete nor truly competitive without a strong bench. Those players who possibly have not started yet are showing up at practice, pushing the starters, and making the team better, and substituting in games as needed, are an essential and valued component of any accomplished squad. At times an unsung player on the team develops their game and develops confidence and steps up and makes an increased and needed positive impact. Or sometimes a new student, an athletically talented player, moves into the area, attends the school, and joins the team.

Fortunately, for the 1965 Team, a new player moved into the Ashe Central school district and provided a missing link for the Panthers at the right time. Teammate John Jackson recounts, "David Mullis spent his elementary years alternating between Jefferson and schools in Texas. His last year at Jefferson was sixth grade. He attended his freshman and sophomore years in Nacona, Texas, where he was an exceptional athlete. He transferred to Ashe Central his junior year, making All-Northwest in basketball."

Player Lanney Blevins concurs on the David Mullis acquisition, "David returned to Jefferson in the summer of 1964. I would often go to his house to play basketball. He played high school ball in Texas through his sophomore year, where he had high scoring and rebounding averages. I shared with him that if he averaged at least ten points and ten rebounds per game we had a decent chance at winning a state championship. He did, and we did!"

Yet another challenge for public high school sports is that typically the varsity team is only together for two years. Most players, with a few exceptions, are members of the varsity squad for their junior and senior years only. Two years is not a lot of time to enculturate players into a coach's system of play. Often by the time eleventh and twelfth grade student-players begin to truly grasp and skillfully execute the team style and strategies, two seasons have hurried by, and graduation is just around the corner.

Coach Rose birthed and nurtured a long-term team vision. This bold and unique vision would begin with seventh and eighth grade students and end with these same players playing varsity basketball together. In place of the usual and customary team term of two years, this core group of cagers would be a unit for six years. As these elementary students transfer to Ashe Central High School, Wade Rose transfers with them. What are the odds of assembling a group of young boys, beginning to shape them into a cohesive unit, including the practice of fundamentals, developing healthy habits, and fostering relational chemistry for six years? The ordinary athletic team obstacles discussed above were being addressed and even overcome through a purposeful and persistent pro-active plan.

THE ODDS OF WINNING MULTIPLE CLOSE GAMES

The odds of going through an entire twenty-game season without a loss are very slim. The 1965 team almost pulled it off. They ended the 1964-1965 regular season with nineteen wins against only one loss. Even that was an amazing feat, beating basketball odds of a single loss over the course of a complete season.

There is much truth in the statement, "We create our own good fortune." It applies to life and to sports. We do have some control over our success with the implementation of good habits and the practice of wise decisions. However, at times situations are out of our control. The statement is likewise true which expresses, "That's just the way the ball bounces." Sometimes in basketball that is literally the case. The ball bounces out of bounds in a tight game, and perhaps this turnover causes the team to lose the game. Or an official makes a controversial call with the game on the line, and your team comes up on the short end. Perhaps one of the starters on the team, who practices good health habits, yet consumes some tainted food which causes food poisoning, and due to this unforeseen illness, he cannot play in a key contest. He misses the game, and the team greatly misses his normal contributions, because of an innocent decision to eat a meal. These situations, and more, are part and parcel of an average year for all teams.

Given all these possible sports scenarios listed in this chapter, and more, it is no wonder that very few teams finish a season undefeated, or even with only a couple losses over an entire schedule. Yet the '65 Panthers were able to accomplish a near perfect season with only one contest in the lost column.

Winning becomes even more impressive, and more high-pressure, in the postseason, as usually the competition is stronger, with the strongest teams advancing and playing one another. The odds of winning a state championship become even smaller in postseason because it is a "one and done" scenario. If a team loses only one game, they exit the tournament.

Defeating the odds in the District Tournament, which consisted of three games, Ashe Central pulled off not one, but two, two-point victories on their march to the championship. This was a team which seemed to get only stronger in the face of challenging obstacles and more determined to overcome overwhelming odds each step of the championship journey.

ATTITUDE

Maintaining a good attitude is a continual challenge for a team. If the team experiences a losing streak, it can be difficult to keep a positive morale. On the other hand, if a team continues winning game after game, the attitude can be a posture of overconfidence. Either extreme is dangerous.

As a former high school coach, I recall our basketball team, which had just won several consecutive games, beginning to display a different, and dangerous, persona. The players were not their usual self. They were bragging, unlike in the past. They also were not working as hard in practice. The next couple of games we lost. We had a team meeting. Out of this meeting of the minds we developed a motto which we verbalized and utilized prior to each game for the rest of that season. The motto: Confidence, not cockiness.

ACHS continued to win game after game. Confidence was on display. It was displayed by maintaining a hunger to win coupled with a strong work ethic. Cockiness was kept in check through a realization that if they let down their guard they could be defeated. Perhaps the only loss to North Wilkes, happening during the regular season, served to remind the team of this reality. Should they become complacent their bold season vision would be in jeopardy. And this single loss also may well have served to take the proverbial monkey off their backs. Sometimes after winning a long string of games and maintaining an undefeated record can bring a lot of pressure. Paradoxically, losing a game can take some pressure off the team and bring the players back down to earth, potentially enabling them to loosen up and play even stronger, better basketball.

SMALL SCHOOL, SMALL COUNTY

Of the eight teams in the 1965 North Carolina 2A State Tournament Ashe Central High School was the second smallest school. Many of the schools in the tournament had much larger student enrollment. Several of these larger schools were located near urban areas where there existed more athletic facilities, sporting events and resources contrasted with more remote areas, such as a small, mountainous community.

The odds are against a relatively small school, in a more rural, isolated and agricultural area winning a state championship. Yet with a bold vision, an unusually gifted coaching duo, and talented, committed players, the small high school from the mountains stayed focused on the cherished vision, persevering through obstacles, and coming out as champions!

THE OBSTACLE OF ALL OBSTACLES

Before concluding this chapter on challenges, we consider now the greatest and most tragic obstacle which the 1965 Team faced. This was an overwhelming challenge and a devastating loss which no team ever expects to endure. This was the obstacle of all obstacles encountered by the Panthers. The '65 Team was confronted by the grave illness and eventual death of their head coach, Coach Wade Rose.

Coach Rose's last game on the team bench was the Beaver Creek game at Beaver Creek, January 26th, 1965. It was the final time he could muster enough energy and strength to be there for and with the team in person. The players had realized Coach was sick, but until this point in time they did not know the severity of his illness. Earlier in the season, one of the team members was playing one-on-one with Coach Rose following practice. At one point the Coach's shirt lifted and the player saw a tube attached to Wade's body. Heretofore, Rose had not informed the team of this mode of medical treatment he was undergoing, which provided a frequent supply of antibiotics to his cancerous liver. Coach Rose continued actively coaching the team as long as he possibly could. Now, due to his debilitating disease, he could no longer pull it off.

How would the team respond to Coach Rose's severe illness? He was their Coach who had conceived and nurtured a vision that had become contagious to the players. He had tutored them and guided many of them since the seventh grade. What would be their response to the two months of games remaining without their head coach? How would things work out, now with Assistant Coach Walker at the helm? There existed so many questions and there were provided so few answers.

But Coach's health was deteriorating rapidly. His energy was depleted. Beginning in January of 1965 he was barely able to walk on his own strength. Hospital stays were now more frequent during the winter of '65. Over the course of Rose's illness, he was hospitalized many times.

The team traversed through two months of ballgames without their beloved head coach. Assistant Coach Morris Walker had now stepped into the role of coaching the team. How would the final portion of the season end for the Panthers?

PLAYER REFELCTIONS ON TEAM OBSTACLES

Our game at Beaver Creek High School was the last game that Coach Rose coached. It was a hard game that we barely won. Coach Walker then stepped up and we did not miss a beat. – Lanney Blevins

Winning a state championship is a major accomplishment for any team. We were considered by most other schools as a group of "hillbillies" from the mountains who had no chance of being successful in the tournament. The fans for the opponents were very vocal and predicted that we would be going home after our first game with Stedman. Hearing those comments only made our team closer and more determined to show everyone that we could play ball with anyone. – David Mullis

Our competitive hurdle was to get past North Wilkes High School. Of course, West Wilkes was another strong opponent who played very well against us in the semi-finals. But North was the continually competitive team at a consistently high level. They only lost two games in the '64-'65 season, both to Ashe Central. – John Jackson

The hurdle to overcome was when our beloved Coach Rose was sick and diagnosed with lung and liver cancer. This was a huge obstacle, but this caused our team to pull together like no other team, playing for our dying coach. – Michael Badger

CAR LICENSE PLATE OF PANTHERS

Chapter 6

THE GAMES

"The district tournament was more challenging than the state tournament." - Player John Jackson

The '64-'65 Panthers finished the regular season with an impressive nineteen wins against only one loss. Their only loss of the entire season came at the hands of their arch-rival, the North Wilkes Vikings. North defeated Ashe Central on their home floor, in Wilkes County, on December 11th, 1964, by a score of 48 to 43. On January 8th, 1965, the Panthers got revenge by beating the Vikings on their home court, 74 to 66.,

Historically, North Wilkes had a very strong basketball program, and this season was no exception. Panther player John Jackson reminisces, "It would have likely taken an act of God to beat North Wilkes at Trap Hill! Central seemingly never got a fair shake at North Wilkes. Their fans were rabid. The principal led the school's alma mater between junior varsity and varsity games. And the officiating was obviously lopsided. Then on top of everything, Coach Rose, who stayed composed, received an undeserved technical foul!"

North Wilkes was competitive. They were confident. And they received a bit of "home cooking" from the officials. All this, and more, made it almost impossible to beat them on their own floor. The Vikings also had experienced being crowned State 2AA Champs only a few seasons prior, in 1961. They had tasted the ultimate victory, and they were not easily denied a repeat journey to the finals. However, Ashe Central would have something to say, and to do, about North Wilkes seeking to outlast and oust them during 1965 post-season.

The regular season North Wilkes loss seemed to serve as a team reminder. A reality check. The Panthers were not invincible and if they were to pursue their goal, they had better not get slack and complacent. During the months of January and February of '65 the team stayed focused and soundly defeated opponents by ten to twenty points, and several games were won by an even greater margin. With one exception: the cross-county rival, the Beaver Creek Beavers, put a scare into Ashe Central.

The Panthers loved to get up and down the floor quickly. Transition basketball suited their players' style and ability very well. On January 26th, 1965, Beaver Creek designed and executed a smart game plan. They would slow down the pace of the game. They implemented a stall tactic. This was the day prior to any shot clock. Teams could maintain possession if they managed to keep the ball away from the defense. This deliberate, slow down, pace kept the Panthers off kilter. At the end of quarter one the scoreboard read, Ashe Central 3, Beaver Creek 2. At halftime the Panthers were in the lead 11 to 4. During the third period the two teams played almost evenly. When this quarter concluded, Ashe Central was ahead 25 to 17.

In the fourth and final quarter Beaver Creek began hitting shots and Central not so much. The Beavers outscored the Panthers 17 to 10 in the last period. The final score: Ashe Central 35; Beaver Creek 34! This was also the last time Coach Wade Rose would be on the Panthers' bench. The illness was taking its toll. Ashe Central had barely escaped the Beaver gym with only a one-point victory. And now their beloved head coach was no longer able to be with them at their games. Two wake-up calls for the Panthers. One courtesy of the Beavers. The other due to the horrible disease cancer. The Panthers were awakened! For the six remaining games of the regular season no opponents' final score was closer than ten points!

In the absence of Wade Rose, Assistant Coach Morris Walker was now coaching the team from the sidelines. The motivation factor of playing for their "sixth man" – Coach Rose – coupled with their sobering scare at the hands of Beaver Creek High School, yielded an Ashe Central team that possessed a renewed drive and determination.

64 ASHE CENTRAL 65
BASKETBALL SCHEDULE
Dec. 1 — West Wilkes, home
Dec. 4 — Lansing, home
Dec. 8 — Beaver Creek, home
Dec. 11 — North Wilkes, away
Dec. 15 — Appalachian, home
Dec. 18 — Surry Central, home
CHRISTMAS HOLIDAY
DOUBLEHEADER
Dec. 30 — Hiddenite, home
Dec. 31 — Maiden, home
Jan. 1 — Open
Jan. 5 — ~~Open~~ LANSING, AWAY
Jan. 8 — North Wilkes, home
Jan. 12 — Elkin, away
Jan. 15 — West Wilkes, away
Jan. 19 — East Wilkes, away
Jan. 22 — Appalachian, away
Jan. 26 — Beaver Creek, away
Jan. 29 — North Surry, home
Feb. 2 — Open
Feb. 5 — Elkin, home
Feb. 9 — Surry Central, away
Feb. 12 — North Surry, home
Feb. 16 — East Wilkes, home
Feb. 19 — ~~Lansing, away~~

game schedule

This image is a blown-up scan of the original
1964/65 game schdule on display is in this case.

ACHS '64-'65 SCHEDULE

THE DISTRICT 7AA TOURAMENT

On March 4th, 1965, Ashe Central played its initial game in the district 7AA tournament against Bunker Hill High School. The district tournament was hosted by Elkin High School. Dale Phillips was the referee and Don Pardue was the umpire for the Ashe Central – Bunker Hill game.

Ashe jumped out to an early 17-13 lead. At halftime it was a one-point game, with the Panthers ahead 25-24. The third quarter Panther positive performance gave them a bit of breathing room, as they outscored Bunker Hill 20 to 12. The teams played almost evenly in the final quarter, with Ashe scoring 14 and Bunker putting 16 on the scoreboard. David Mullis led all scorers with twenty-two points and nine rebounds. Bob Francis contributed a double-double with twenty points and ten rebounds. The final score: Ashe Central – 59; Bunker Hill – 52. Ashe Central advanced to the second round of the district tournament.

In the second round on March 5th, the Panthers faced a familiar opponent from their own conference, namely West Wilkes. Central had defeated West twice in the regular season. It is difficult to beat a team twice in a season. To win three times over the same opponent is even more difficult. The table was set for a heated rematch. Henry Brown was the referee and S. S. Wilson the umpire.

West Wilkes came out fired up and on fire with their accurate outside shooting. The Black Hawks scored sixteen points, to Ashe Central's five points, in the first quarter. The Panthers began the game in a 3-2 zone defense, switching to a 1-3-1 zone, then transitioning to man-to-man, to stop the outside scoring of West. In the second quarter ACHS outscored West Wilkes by one point, 14 to 13, with the Panthers trailing 19 to 29 at the half.

A portion of Coach Walker's game notes includes, "We adjusted by coming out of our zone and our man-to-man defense looked good. Our offense was chiefly overload getting the ball in to the low post. Osborne (high scorer for West Wilkes) got four fouls, so we worked the ball to the man he was guarding (Mullis). Our man-to-man defense got us moving and enabled our offense to improve. We shot 81% during the second half and made 88% of our free throws."

After a halftime discussion and strategic plan, the Panthers went to work in the third period. At the end of the third quarter the game was tied, 40 to 40! The fourth quarter was an offensive battle, with Ashe scoring twenty points and West scoring eighteen. During this final period point guard Charlie Bowers provided eight points, including six for six from the free throw line, giving him seventeen points in the game.

Bob Francis added twenty-three points and eleven boards. Mullis scored thirteen points with six rebounds. The Panthers had survived a close one. Ashe Central advanced. Their reward? They would face their nemesis, North Wilkes, in the district championship game. Nothing got easier!

This would be the third game in as many nights. Ashe Central and North Wilkes had split regular season games, with each team winning on their respective home floor. Now had arrived the rubber game of the match and on a neutral court. Which team would bring the strategy and the stamina to perform as the superior squad? The two teams lined up at center court for the jump ball, the referee was Dale Phillips, the umpire, Don Pardue.

Both teams started the game slowly with each scoring a relatively low eight points. The first half concluded with Central leading, 19 to 16. North's game plan was to slow the pace. A slower, very deliberate style of play continued in the second half. At the end of the third period Ashe Central held a 32 to 26 advantage. During the final quarter North outscored the Panthers 14 to 10. With seconds left in the game a North player scored a bucket to come within two points of Ashe Central. A foul was also called on the play for a potential three-point play. The Vikings elected for an intentional miss at the free throw line. Somehow North managed to grab the offensive rebound with seconds remaining in regulation play. North next called a time out. Lanney Blevins recalls, "In the regional finals we were ahead by two points with little time to go. North Wilkes had the ball and called a timeout. Coach Walker said not to foul Gambill. He got the ball on the in-bounds pass. All five of us surrounded him with our hands extended upward. No foul was called, and we won the game!" The final score read, Ashe Central – 42, North Wilkes – 40.

Walker's game notes included, "We ran the best 1-3-1 match-up zone I have seen this year by this team. David Pell did an exceptional job of running the backside of the zone. North ran man-to-man so we worked the ball into the low post. A close game between two great teams. We were fortunate to come out on top and advance to the state tournament!"

What a close, hard-fought game between two talented and fierce rivals! Ashe Central had prevailed in the district tournament! The Panthers were going to the North Carolina State Tournament! Coach Rose's vision was still alive! Although his physical presence was not on the bench or at the games, his influence and impact was certainly felt!

THE STATE AA TOURNAMENT

Ashe Central High School was going to the state playoffs! The excitement in the hallways at Central, and throughout campus, was palpable. Students and teachers were visibly pumped for the Panthers team. This post-season tournament milestone was a rarity for any team. Many were making plans to travel to Winston-Salem to support the squad in their quest for a state championship.

There was much preparation necessary to get ready for the upcoming trip. Personal schedules were altered. Bus rides were planned. Team travel logistics must be arranged. And amidst all the excitement and distractions the team had to remain focused on their game and on their goal. The squad only had a couple days of practice to prepare for their next opponent. Being crowned district champions was wonderful, but this was not the time to prolong a celebration. The Panthers plans were not completed. The mission continued. The vision was still alive. Staying focused on their game, with each player concentrating on his role, had gotten the team this far. It was this same focus and concentration that was required for the state tournament.

To be successful there must be much attention given to details. A page from Coach Walker's calendar, including the 1965 dates of Monday, March 8th through Sunday, March 14th, contains the following:

Monday, March 8th –

Get uniforms to Mrs. Sheets (cleaned and pressed)

Call The Skyland Post, State Tournament Information

Call WKSK, State Tournament Information

Motivational speaker at practice today

Tuesday, March 9th –

13 players will travel (one injured)

2 team managers

Arrange hotel room assignments.

Pack all the equipment.

Gas activity bus

Take food money for team meals.

Pep rally at 2:30pm

Wednesday, March 10th

8:15am Leave for State AA Tournament

Check-in at the Sheraton Motor Inn, Winston-Salem

Uniforms packed (black and white)

Towels

First aid kit

Practice uniforms

Each player takes:

- Clothing
- Towels
- Clean athletic socks
- Toiletry items
- Practice uniforms
- Tennis shoes

Thursday, March 11th

The Ashe Central team works out at Wake Forest University in the afternoon.

In the evening the Panthers do some scouting, as they watch the Anson County team in action.

Early on the morning of Wednesday, March 10th, 1965, the Panthers boarded the activity bus at Lee Bower's Store. Soon they would be bound for Winston-Salem to check into their hotel, then eat a pre-game meal prior to their opening game in the state tournament. They were paired with Stedman High School at Reynolds High School in Winston-Salem, North Carolina, where all the State AA Tournament games would be played.

Yet, prior to their leaving the county, there was a priority stop to make. The team bus was driven directly to the home of Wade and Gwen Rose! The Panthers gathered around the Coach in his home. It was a tender time, as the now thin, fragile Coach Rose gave them some words of encouragement and sent them off to the State Tournament. The one who had instilled a vision within them six years prior; the coach who had taught, inspired and guided them all along, was now forced to remain behind. As the team reboarded the bus not a dry eye was found.

Upon arriving in Winston-Salem, the players were given their hotel room assignments and checked into their respective rooms. Not long afterward the team would walk across the hotel parking lot to the K and W Cafeteria for their pre-game meal. This was where they would eat their team meals while in Winston. The North Carolina High School Athletic Association provided a per diem of $1.25 each day for meals for up to twelve players (Factoring for inflation, $1.25 in 1965 is worth about $12.25 in today's currency). Regarding their meals, player Michael Badger reflects, "We ate all our meals at the K and W Cafeteria on Stratford Road, next to the Sheraton Inn, where we were staying during the tournament. One of our players had never eaten at a cafeteria, nor had he been out of Ashe County. The teammate saw the wide variety of good food and he particularly loved potatoes. He got mashed potatoes, French fries, and scalloped potatoes all on his tray!"

After the meal it was time to go back to their rooms at the hotel for a time of rest and centering upon the upcoming contest, prior to travelling to Reynolds High School for their opening game with Stedman.

STATE AA TOURNAMENT, ROUND ONE

Ashe Central High and Stedman High squared off at Reynold's High School Gymnasium in round one of the North Carolina AA Tournament on March 10th, 1965, with Frank Murry and Sam Hudson officiating.

In the initial period of play, Ashe scored 17 points to 11 points for Stedman. In the second quarter the Panthers started pulling away, outscoring their opponent 19 to 12. At halftime the scoreboard read, Ashe Central – 36, Stedman – 23.

Following halftime Stedman High came out showing more intensity than evidenced in the first half. They outscored Central 17 to 13 in the third quarter, resulting in a 49 to 40 lead by the Panthers going into the final quarter. The fourth quarter belonged to Ashe, as they outscored their opponent 20 to 15. Ashe Central had won the opening round of the state tournament by a score of 69 to 55.

David Mullis put up a huge double-double, scoring thirty points and bringing down twenty-three rebounds. With the tandem towers of Francis and Mullis, teams had a very difficult time handling both big men. If they doubled down on one man, the other player could dominate.

The Panthers had so many weapons. Each position was talent-ladened and if one player was off on any night, another player would step up and come through for the team. Unselfish team play and balanced scoring, along with athleticism and solid defense made for a winning formula for the '65 Panthers. On the other side of the ball, Stedman relied far too much upon only one player, their big 6' 9" man in the middle. The Stedman center did score twenty-one points, but he couldn't do it all by himself. In contrast, ACHS had several players who contributed scoring at critical points in the game to augment Mullis' excellent offensive performance. Balanced scoring through multiple players throughout the entire season provided resiliency and team consistency, proving to be a Panthers' winning formula.

John Jackson shares, "David Mullis had a field day, scoring thirty points. His picture appeared in the next day's Winston-Salem Journal. The Journal article covering the Ashe Central – Stedman game included a quotation from fans' conversation in the gym lobby. Two men were overheard talking about the Panthers. 'The key to beating Central,' one said, 'is to focus on Francis, number 50.' To which the other fellow responded, 'Then what the hell are we supposed to do with Mullis?'" The Panthers were hitting on all cylinders. Their momentum and confidence were peaking at the right time. They were advancing to the State AA Tournament semi-finals!

STATE AA TOURNAMENT SEMI-FINAL

Ashe Central faced Havelock High School on Friday, March 12th, in the tournament semi-final game. Murry and Brown were the officials. Earlier it was stated how Central had balanced scoring from multiple players. This game would prove no different.

Havelock jumped out to an early lead, as the first quarter ended in their favor, 15 to 14. In the second quarter the Panthers came to life, led by David Pell Bower with 10 points in the second period. David Mullis added six points and Roger Howell also contributed six points. The halftime deficit for Havelock was twelve points. They would never catch Central. The Panthers had found their grove. They were turning it on!

As alluded to earlier, someone stepped up for Ashe when there was a need. This night belonged to Roger Howell, who stepped up his game in a big way! As before, Central's same balanced scoring was in place against Havelock High. David Pell ended the game with twenty-one points. Bob Francis also put in twenty-one. But on this night "hot hand Howell" posted twenty-three points!

Coach Walker and the team had created yet another offensive weapon. Walker knew Howell was a natural shooter, so he placed him on the perimeter instead of in the post. He was in a different position and with a different perspective. Instead of playing with his back to the basket, he was now facing the rim. Roger rose to the challenge, and it paid big dividends for the team. With Howell's perimeter shooting success, Havelock could not play a collapse defense on the Panther's big men.

Many years after winning the 1965 championship, Howell wrote a message to Morris Walker. That letter follows:

Dear Coach Walker,

I remember the night in Winston-Salem in the basketball semi-finals of the state championship game. You started me out on the wing, a position I have never played before in a game. I was so nervous; you'll never know how nervous I was. You said, "Roger, shoot the ball. I know you can. If you don't, I'm taking you out." When the game started, we got the tip and Charlie flipped the ball my way. I was wide open. I thought, "Oh, no!" I was so nervous I flipped the ball back to Charlie, and I saw you out of the corner of my eye. You jumped up and hollered, "Roger!" Charlie passed the ball back, I looked at the goal, and it looked like the size of an aspirin and 90 feet away! I saw you stand up again, so I nervously shot…swish! I could not believe it. I was so thrilled! Next trip down the court, same thing. This went on about five trips down the court. They called time-out, and as I walked to our bench, I saw you looking at me with a big smile on your face. This gave me all the confidence I needed.

A Friend Always,

Roger Howell

Several years ago, prior to Roger's death, in an interview with Josh Beckworth, he recalls, "Coach Walker had to pressure me to shoot from the wing position. Charlie would throw the ball to me, per Coach's orders, but I would pass it right back to Charlie. This went on a few times until Coach Walker jumped off the bench and demanded that I shoot, since the defense was sagging way off me, so they could stop our inside game. I shot and hit. I think I hit three long shots in a row. Heck, now I was feeling it. So, the fourth trip down the floor to our basket, I began asking for the ball!"

Coach Walker's post-game notes included, "We played man-to-man except on player #11, and we told Charlie to let him go and play a sagging, helping defense. Havelock played in a 2-3 and a 2-1-2 zone. We hit from the outside and the inside. Mullis and Francis broke to the high post at different times, running a high-low set. Roger and David Pell hit from the outside. We shot 54%, so now we are in the state championship game!"

The Panthers proved to be too much for Havelock. They went on to win by a score of 90 to 76. The dream was alive! Ashe Central High School was going to the State AA Championship game!

Bob Francis working in the post.

David Mullis, Roger Howell and Charlie Bowers watch the ball bounce out of bounds.

Mullis and Bower double team opponent.

Roger Howell pulls down rebound.

Charlie Bowers dives to the floor.

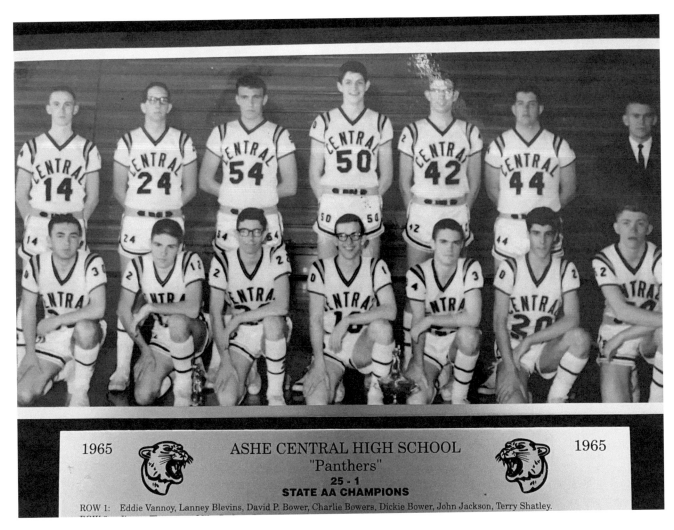

1965   ASHE CENTRAL HIGH SCHOOL   1965
"Panthers"
25 - 1
STATE AA CHAMPIONS
ROW 1:   Eddie Vannoy, Lanney Blevins, David P. Bower, Charlie Bowers, Dickie Bower, John Jackson, Terry Shatley.

1965 State 2A Champions

CHAPTER 7

A DREAM REALIZED

"The 1965 team taught me that anything is possible when good people come together and work toward a common goal and never give up." – Bob Francis

Ashe Central advanced to the finals of the State Tournament by defeating both of their first two opponents, on Thursday and Friday night, by fourteen points. Their opposition for the State AA Championship game on Saturday, March 13th, was Anson County High School. Frank Murry was referee for the game, and Red Wilson, the umpire. Each team was invited to select one official for the game. Ashe Central requested Wilson. Red had officiated Central previously in a regular season game, and he remarked to some of the Panther players that he would see them later in the State Tournament. Wilson must have had a good eye for spotting winning talent! Red would later go on to become the head football coach at Duke University.

The championship game opened with a lot of offense. Both teams put an abundance of points on the board. At the conclusion of the first period Central was in the lead, 25 to 20. John Jackson reflects, "The two teams traded baskets left and right for several minutes. The two squads appeared evenly matched. However, in the second quarter ACHS began to pull steadily ahead, and they were never threatened after that. Coach Walker had encouraged Roger Howell to shoot because Anson would no doubt sag on Mullis and Francis. Roger took the first shot of the game and hit nothing but net! It was a good omen."

There was a moment of suspense for the Panthers when David Mullis received a severe injury and had to leave the game. Mullis got hit in the face. Action was stopped. Ashe County physician, Dr. Dean C. Jones, Jr., attended the game. Jones ushered David to the locker room. He treated Mullis by packing gauze and placing some butterfly strips on the wound. David returned to the game.

At halftime, Ashe Central had 48 points to Anson County's 29. The third quarter was played almost evenly, the Panthers scoring 18, Anson putting up 21 points. With the fourth quarter underway, and ACHS possessing a commanding 66 to 50 lead, the Central team was not to be denied. They had come too far to turn back now! The Panther machine was running on all cylinders. The estimated fifteen-hundred Ashe County citizens who had attended the championship game were breaking out loud and wild with cheers! After a long, tough season the goal had finally been reached! And accomplished in a confident and convincing style! The final score: Ashe Central – 85, Anson County – 68.

The boys from the hills had prevailed! And they had prevailed in a grand manner, beating each of their three state tournament opponents by an average of fifteen points. As Eddie Vannoy states it, "During the state tournament the opposing team had big posters up on the gym wall that contained pictures of outhouses with big half-moons in the doors. I guess they thought we were a bunch of hillbillies, but we took care of business! Before the game was over the posters were taken down because of the score." The opponents' posters came down, and taking their place on the gymnasium wall was an ACHS winning banner which stated in big, bold letters: WE'RE IT – STATE CHAMPIONS THAT IS!

The second period proved to be the permanent turnaround for the Panthers. Ashe Central made second-quarter adjustments which enabled them to gain a big lead. Coach Walker, in his game notes, put it this way, "We started the game in a 1-3-1 zone, but we later switched to our man-to-man defense for the rest of the way. It was a very effective defense. It also enabled our transition offense to get going. We got our five-man offensive fastbreak cranked up and we ran with Anson. It was a great team effort. We are state champions!"

As in previous Panther contests, once again a different player steps up to help with the scoring load. In this game point guard Charlie Bowers scored twenty-one points, shooting 5 of 9 from the field and making 11 out of 13 free throws. Francis netted 24 points. David Pell Bower and David Mullis both contributed 13 points. Howell had 8 points. Larry Cockerham added 4 points and Eddie Vannoy scored 2 points, for a total of 85 team points. The Panthers were beasts on the boards, controlling both ends. Francis brought down 16 rebounds, Mullis grabbed 15, and Howell collected 8.

The Ashe Central Panthers finished the season, the post-season tournaments, and now this final state championship game in a strong, commanding fashion! It had happened! The Panthers had won the North Carolina State AA Championship in boys' basketball! The championship dream had become reality! What a storybook, incredible season! Nineteen wins against one loss in regular season play. Followed by a District

Tournament Championship, with two exciting and exhausting games won by merely two points. Followed by the State AA Championship game victory, which yielded a twenty-five-and-one record! The Panthers had completed the mission! Every practice. Every lap ran. Every play. Every game. Every obstacle. Every effort was worth it all!

It had all begun with a young coach by the name of Wade Rose who had a clear vision of what could transpire if a core group of young boys stuck together for six years, trained in fundamentals, worked hard, and refused to quit through victory or adversity. What began as a seeded vision in 1960, became a jubilant harvest in 1965. Rose reached out to encourage and empower young athletes. Eddie Vannoy fondly remembers, "Coach Rose came down to Nathans Creek Elementary when I was in the seventh grade and started organizing basketball. Before that there was no organized basketball at Nathans Creek. As we got older, on the weekend the players would go to his house and play games and have cookouts instead of running up and down the roads in automobiles. I believe that was a lot of what brought our team together."

The entire Panther squad had caught, and bought, this winning vision from an amazing person who just happened to also be their coach. Wade Rose, along with his wife Gwen, cared for, guided, and even often fed these boys over all their years together, many of them over the course of six years. This team did not only play ball together, but they also did life together. Dickie Bower reflects, "I still think about all the time Coach Rose spent with us and all the experiences we had together with him. He loved the Lord; his family and he loved us."

Again, from Bower, "All of us guys who grew up in Jefferson during the 7th and 8th grades, and beyond, it is no telling what we may have gotten into if Wade Rose had not returned home after college and started teaching and coaching at Jefferson Elementary! Coach Rose started a game and recreation program at the gym and playground. We had never been around anyone like him and he was a big part of our lives until the day he died. You could fill a book with all the hours and experiences he shared with us. What a great example he set for everyone! He often had us at his house. We spent so much time at his home that I don't know how Mrs. Rose stood it. But she was always very welcoming and kind to all of us."

Coach Rose had adopted these players into his life and shaped them into a championship team. He came into their lives early on, while they were still in elementary school. Yet, due to the horrible, cruel disease known as cancer, he likewise left them way too early. He had battled with this sickness for years. He was able to mask and fight it and continue with his coaching responsibilities for a long while. But the terrible illness finally caught up with him. As was mentioned earlier, the Beaver Creek game, at BCHS, on January 26th, 1965, was the final time Rose would be coaching in person on the bench. Following this game Coach Rose spent much of his time on a hospital bed instead of on a gymnasium bench. In fact, he was admitted to the hospital sixteen times from 1963 until his death in 1965. The cancer was taking a huge toll. He was getting much weaker.

The team members now began to comprehend that their beloved Coach was very sick. Over the next six weeks the team members would be playing extra hard, giving their all for what Coach Walker had named, "our sixth man" (Coach Wade Rose). As Badger had stated earlier, "When Coach Rose was sick, diagnosed with lung and liver cancer, that made our team really pull together. We were playing for our dying Coach!" Jimmy Thompson concurs, "Adversity came with Coach Rose's illness. We wanted so badly to win the state championship for him. We were serious, focused, and we worked very hard to make this happen for him."

On the night of the Panther's state championship victory, Coach Rose was at home in the presence of his beloved Gwen. The next morning, he would be admitted as a patient to Ashe Memorial Hospital, far too weak to remain at home. Michael Badger shares about his dad, James Badger, owner and operator of Badger Funeral Home (In this era, prior to EMS, Ashe County utilized the funeral home personnel and vehicles to transport patients when needed) devising a plan for Coach Rose, "My Dad was going to bring Coach Rose to Winston-Salem, to Reynolds High School Gym, on a cot to be on our bench during the game. But Coach was too weak to make the transport and Dad called the hotel to tell me that Coach Rose was too sick to travel."

While Wade Rose was too frail to travel, and even too sick to carry on a conversation, nonetheless eighty-six miles northwest of Winston-Salem, lying in his bed at home, Coach Rose and Gwen were listening to the championship game via radio. Gwen remembers clearly, "During the game on March 13th, Wade was at home where we kept him as comfortable as possible. He was in and out of a coma during the game. As we listened on the radio to the final minutes of the game, Wade knew the team had won. He grinned, as the final buzzer sounded, and with as much energy as he could muster, he raised both his fists in the air! His last words were, 'They did it!' I raised my hands along with Wade, and we celebrated the victory together. The next morning, we had him transferred to Ashe Memorial Hospital."

The architect of an awesome athletic accomplishment was gratefully and graciously able to see the completion of his building – team building! From a limited human perspective, it was a devastating tragedy to lose a person before he even reached the relatively young age of thirty. No doubt, this loss was crushing.

It seemed so unfair. It appeared so untimely. There was so much life to live and basketball to play! Yet, amid the grief, how beautiful for Coach Rose to see the final fruition of his long-time vision being fulfilled! On his deathbed he was able to smile, celebrate and lift his hands in victory!

The game was played and won. And the earthly race had been run. The Coach had courageously battled cancer. Now he was tired and worn. He was ready to go to his eternal home. Gwen affirmed, "Wade taught us how to live as a Christian, and he taught us how to die as a Christian." The words of scripture come to mind, "I have fought the good fight. I have finished the race. I have kept the faith. Now there waits for me the crown of righteousness which the Lord, the Righteous Judge, will award me on that day" (2 Timothy 4:7,8. NIV). As fabulous as a state championship is, it pales in comparison to the crown of righteousness which Coach Rose received. Talk about a victory trophy!

Wade Rose left a legacy and a positive impact. Some people, just because of who they are, make the world a better place. Coach Rose was one of those helpful personas. He gave of himself to make others better. He did not only develop players, but he also cultivated individuals. Dickie Bower adds, "He had the vision. He was the leader. He loved people. God knew what he was doing in and through Wade Rose. He was changing our lives! Changing many lives for the better."

Although the basketball vision was fulfilled and the championship dream became reality, a stark and sobering reality set in with the death of Coach Rose. On Saturday night the team members were game-winning ball players. On Wednesday morning they were grief-stricken pall bearers. As Charlie Bowers puts it, "It was a sorrowful time. We went from winning the title Saturday to serving as pall bearers at Coach's funeral on Wednesday."

Less than a day and a half, approximately thirty hours, following the championship game, a bit prior to 6AM, Charlie Bowers was opening his dad's store in East Jefferson, and he received the sobering news, "Coach Rose, has just passed away!" On the other side of Jefferson, just a few minutes later, Michael Badger recalls, "My dad woke me up at 6AM on Monday, March 15th, to tell me, 'I just picked up your Coach this morning to take him to the funeral home. I'm sorry, Michael, he's gone.'"

From the pen of John Jackson we read, "The 1965 State AA Championship very much belonged to Coach Wade Rose. Although he had fought cancer for three years, and coached even when he did not feel well, the 1965 Team was his. He died just a little over one day after the victory, while hospitalized at Ashe Memorial. After Central's victory over Anson County, the Winston-Salem Journal's sports headline read,

"Ashe Wins Title for Dying Coach." Coach Walker saw the article early on Sunday morning, as the team was at the bowling alley. Out of compassion and courtesy he telephoned Gwen as quickly as he could to give her a heads-up on this startling headline, prior to her reading it later that day.

The Ashe Central team, in celebrating their state championship elected to spend Saturday night bowling. They celebrated the awesome win. They had a wonderful time bowling into the early morning hours. Together they experienced much fun and laughter, and certainly a well-deserved time after a long, tough, but victorious, season. Yet now they would see the newspaper, as they read with great interest the reporting about their game. And what they would read would, for certain, put a deep damper on their celebration.

Throughout their extraordinary season the Panthers had known ups and downs. They had known success, goals met, and championships. They had also encountered challenges, hurdles and trials. No wonder athletics has often been compared to life. Life is filled with celebrations and with challenges. For the Central team it was no different. Coach Rose had taught them so much about life and living. Now, in his death, he was teaching them about dying.

In a relatively short span of six years of coaching and mentoring, Wade Rose had left a lasting impact on some very young lives. The sport of basketball had become a vehicle through which life lessons were relayed. The team members were not just better players, because of their relationships with Coach Rose, they had become better people.

The words of poet P. T. Berkey apply here:

> There are certain people
> who enter our lives
> that help
> to make each and every day
> an exciting adventure
> filled with hope,
> love
> and greatness.
>
>
> These,
> are the type of people

91

who somehow manage

to make everything

feel like

some kind of magic.

These are my people.

A service of death and resurrection was held at the Johnny Luke Memorial Gymnasium at the Glendale Springs Presbyterian Church on the morning of Wednesday, March 17th, at 11am. The March 18th, 1965, edition of The Skyland Post contained the following article:

RITES HELD ON WEDNESDAY FOR D. WADE ROSE, 28

Funeral service was held Wednesday morning for Delmer Wade Rose, 28, who died early Monday morning at the Ashe Memorial Hospital after a long period of serious illness.

The service was held in the Johnny Luke Memorial Building which he had helped to plan.

Conducting the service were Dr. John H. Luke, Dr. R. H. Stone and Rev. John Christy. A burial followed in the Ashelawn Memorial Cemetery. The family requested that instead of flowers, memorial gifts be made to the Ashe Hospital to start a fund for a memorial chapel there.

All schools in the Ashe Central district were closed on Wednesday for the funeral.

He had served as teacher and basketball coach for the past four years at Ashe Central where he was both popular and effective. The Ashe Central team which he coached, won the State 2-A Championship in Winston-Salem Saturday night before their coach died.

Coach Rose, who was stricken with cancer some months ago continued with his work until after Christmas.

He was born November 20, 1936, in Ashe County, the son of Delmer and Helen Lyle Rose.

He graduated from Jefferson High School in 1954 and attended Lees-McRae College at Banner Elk for two years and then went to Catawba College at Salisbury, where he graduated with an A.B degree in 1958.

He was an outstanding basketball player in high school and college.

After graduating from Catawba, he worked a year at Salisbury and then in 1959 came back to Ashe

County. He taught the eighth grade at Jefferson for two years and also coached the boys and girls in basketball there. Then he became head basketball coach at Ashe Central and was there for four years.

He is survived by his wife, Mrs. Gwen Neal Rose; two daughters, Virginia and Mary Rose, and one son, John Rose, all of the home; his parents of Glendale Springs, his paternal grandparents, Mr. and Mrs. Arthur Rose of Glendale Springs, and his maternal grandmother, Mrs. Flossie Lyle of Wagoner.

Active pallbearers were Bob Francis, Michael Badger, Charlie Bowers, David Pell Bower, Lanney Blevins, Roger Howell, and Larry Cockerham, members of the Ashe Central basketball team who worked with Rose since the sixth grade at Jefferson.

Honorary pallbearers were R. O. Jackson, Robert Woodie, Colonel Francis, Kyle Dickson, James Church, and Earl Ruth.

A championship had been won on the basketball court by a team who had followed a head coach, a life mentor, who had loved them and guided them. A competent and caring assistant coach continued carrying the vision which Coach Rose had initiated and integrated into a group of young men's lives. Through coaching guidance, community support, and never giving up on a bold vision, the Panther team had overcome odds and obstacles to obtain a rare, incredible goal! While an awesome, yet temporary, victory had been gained on the court on Saturday, March 13th, 1965, a permanent victory was awarded Wade Rose as he entered his eternal home on Monday, March 15th. May Wade Rose rest in peace and may his memory be a blessing!

During Coach Rose's funeral a group of ACHS students, who had named their singing group, The Charades, sang "Amazing Grace". It seems fitting to close this chapter, as well as the book, with a portion of the lyrics to this timeless and reassuring hymn:

"Amazing Grace, how sweet the sound,

That saved a wretch like me.

I once was lost, but now am found,

Was blind but now I see.

When we've been there ten thousand years,

Bright shining as the sun.

We've no less days to sing God's praise,

Then when we first begun."

The team with state tournament trophy.

The Johnny Luke Memorial Building at Glendale Springs, N C, the site of Coach Rose's funeral.

AFTERWORD

The 1964-1965 men's basketball team was so much more than a group of high school boys who were fortunate enough to win a state championship. Our team was unique in many ways. Almost all of us started playing in the seventh grade under a coach who would not only hone our athletic skills, but also influence our lives forever.

Coach Wade Rose taught us that dedication, discipline, hard work and practice were central to success on and off the court. We were expected to act and look like gentlemen. Coach, as he liked to be called, tempered his high expectations with both humor and kindness, often pulling practical jokes on team members.

As we began the '64-'65 season, the team had grown so cohesive that we practically knew what each of us was thinking. This intuitiveness became central to our success. As the season progressed, both our school and local community rallied around us. We were experiencing a dream season. Then we learned of Coach's illness. He became too sick to coach on the bench with us. His absence could have been an insurmountable obstacle, but it was one we would overcome.

Coach Morris Walker stepped in as our coach, and we renewed our goal to win the state championship, not only for ourselves, but for our dying coach. Under Coach Walker's guidance we succeeded. Our victory on March 13, 1965, was, however, bittersweet. Coach Rose passed away within hours of our winning the state title. Although we were just teenagers when we lost Coach, the values he instilled in us have sustained us throughout our adult lives. I was both honored and humbled to be a part of the '65 Championship Team!

Charlie Bowers, Co-Captain
2023

ABOUT THE AUTHOR

Michael Kurtz possesses a strong affinity for the high country, especially Ashe County, where he was raised by parents, Elam and Orpah Kurtz. Elam S. Kurtz, M.D., was an Ashe County physician who set up a medical practice in the late 1950s, in the town of Lansing, N.C.

He also has a passion for basketball, which was partially lived out through being a part of the following teams: Jefferson Elementary School – 7th and 8th grades ('67-'69); Ashe Central High School ('69-'73) – two years J. V. and two years Varsity; Lees-McRae Junior College ('73-75); and Eastern Mennonite University ('75-'77). After college ball he participated as a player in the Ashe County Industrial League with the Lambert Hawks, who had a legendary team with 100s of wins. Kurtz was also a member of the Ashe County Panthers who played in the N.C. Senior Games in 2015 and 2016, bringing home to Ashe a bronze medal both years.

From 1977 until 1981, Coach Kurtz taught English and coached sports at Northwest Ashe High School in Warrensville, N. C. His coaching at NWA included two years of coaching boys' J.V. basketball and two years of boys' varsity.

In the fall of 1981, Michael and Karen Christy were married at Jefferson United Methodist Church in Jefferson, N.C. That same autumn season, Kurtz enrolled at Duke Divinity School at Duke University, Durham, N.C. Following course work at Duke and pastoral internships at three churches, Kurtz pastored six congregations in a thirty-eight-year career with the United Methodist Church in the Western North Carolina Conference. The congregation locations were Thomasville (6 years); High Point (4 years); Salisbury (5 years); Concord (7 years); Oak Ridge (10 years); Asheville (6 years). At the time of this writing, Pastor Kurtz is serving in a part time, retired WNC status, at the Warrensville UMC Charge (Clifton, Smethport and Warrensville churches).

In 1994, Kurtz received a Doctor of Ministry degree from Eastern Baptist Theological Seminary (Palmer University today). Rev. Kurtz is also a licensed marriage and family therapist (NCLMFT #609), working in this capacity part time in private practice. He began practicing therapy in 1996 and continues working with individuals, couples and families. Kurtz also is a trainer of facilitators for Prepare – Enrich, an international relationship therapy resource.

Michael and Karen are retired to Ashe County. They have two grown children, two grandsons and two grand dogs. Michael enjoys running and hiking and singing with Karen. He also spends his time reading, writing, playing guitar, cooking, yard work, swimming, playing golf and delivering meals-on-wheels.

One of Michael's favorite mantras, and that which he seeks to live by, is that which states, "Agree to disagree, agreeably." Kurtz is convinced that if we all lived by this respectful philosophy and lifestyle, we would experience less divisiveness and more shalom in our world.

Printed in the United States
by Baker & Taylor Publisher Services